The Fountas&Pinnell

Comprehensive Phonics, Spelling, and Word Study Guide

Irene C. Fountas
Gay Su Pinnell

HEINEMANN
Portsmouth, NH

Heinemann
361 Hanover Street
Portsmouth, NH 03801-3912
www.heinemann.com

Offices and agents throughout the world

Cataloging-in-Publication Data is on file with the Library of Congress.
The Fountas & Pinnell Comprehensive Phonics, Spelling, and Word Study Guide
ISBN: 978-0-325-08939-3

Editor: David Pence
Production: Lynne Costa, Angel Lepore
Cover design: Monica Ann Crigler and Suzanne Heiser
Text design: Monica Ann Crigler
Typesetter: Technologies 'N Typography, Inc.
Manufacturing: Deanna Richardson

Printed in the United States of America on acid-free paper
21   20   19   VP   4   5

CONTENTS

Acknowledgments

Acknowledgments

This *Comprehensive Phonics, Spelling, and Word Study Guide* is a meticulously constructed comprehensive picture of the linguistic and language knowledge students develop on their journey to become highly expert and flexible word solvers.

We are especially grateful to David Pence and Kathy Mormile, who brought many long hours of analysis and their excellent ideas to the production of this useful reference for teachers. Their systematic thinking and careful analysis have brought rigor and integrity to the work.

Our Heinemann production staff, including Michael Cirone, Lynne Costa, and Angel Lepore, led this team with their hard work and expertise. We thank Lisa Fowler, Monica Ann Crigler, and Suzanne Heiser for the brilliant cover and interior designs. All of the Heinemann team have worked together to make the continuum a useful tool for teachers.

We could not have produced this volume without the expert assistance of Cheryl Wasserstrom, Sharon Freeman, and Andrea Lelievre. We particularly appreciate their willingness to be flexible and to put in extra effort when needed.

To our publisher, Mary Lou Mackin, we are truly indebted. She is the person who keeps all systems going in the right direction. We also thank Samantha Garon for her creative suggestions and advice as we thought about presenting this work to educators.

Introduction

Introduction

The Fountas & Pinnell Comprehensive Phonics, Spelling, and Word Study Guide is a description of the essential understandings related to the alphabetic system that characterizes English. This volume represents a comprehensive picture of understandings that teachers need to know to understand literacy learners from PreK to middle school. Your teaching may be directed at students of a certain age; however, increasingly we find that it is helpful to a community of teachers to have a "big picture" view of phonics, spelling, and word study.

For one thing, the achievement of this complex set of understandings is very diverse even within one classroom. As you observe your students, you are likely to find that many students need to develop understandings that others in the same class have fully established; some students will be advanced beyond their current grade level, yet almost all students may have missed a key understanding and found themselves confused in the challenges your curriculum poses. Secondly, lifting the literacy abilities of students in your school cannot be fully achieved until teachers work as a collaborative community to take collective responsibility for each cohort. It is valuable to have a view of the complex learning that even very young students take on as they enter school, as well as a view of the high expectations they encounter as they move into middle or high school. At each grade level, you would want an understanding of what went before and what will be coming for your students.

It's important to recognize that, while important, phonics, spelling, word analysis, and grammar and usage strategies are not the end goal of literacy education. Their importance lies in their contribution to reading and writing continuous text. The more that students can solve words, derive the meaning of words, spell words, and parse language syntax rapidly, fluently, and unconsciously, the more likely they are to read and write with competence and ease.

This volume serves as a reference for your work in phonics, spelling, and word study. In it, you will find a series of statements that clearly describe principles related to nine areas of learning (see Figure I-1).

These nine areas offer an approximation of typical learning over time. In interpreting this document, it's important to realize that learners do not change in exactly the same way, but they do build complex learning toward this picture of proficiency.

As you look at the continuum, you will notice that most areas are organized into subcategories and that principles (as embodied in student behaviors) are listed in "teacher language" within each category and subcategory. Along with the statement of the principle, when applicable, you will find examples that will be helpful to you in teaching. (Sometimes it's hard to call to mind specific examples of exactly what you are teaching.) All of this information will

FIGURE I-1 *Developing Word-Solving Systems: Nine Areas of Learning*

Early Literacy Concepts	Early literacy concepts include understandings such as knowing to read from left to right and voice-to-print matching. Many children enter kindergarten with good knowledge of early literacy concepts. If they do not, then explicit and systematic instruction can help them become oriented quickly. While most of these early literacy concepts are not "phonics," they are basic to the child's understanding of print and should be mastered early.
Phonological Awareness	A key to becoming literate is the ability to hear the sounds in words. Hearing individual sounds allows the learner to connect sounds and letters. A general response to the sounds of language is called *phonological awareness.* As learners become more aware of language, they notice sounds in a more detailed way. *Phonemic awareness* involves recognizing the *individual* sounds in words and, eventually, being able to identify, isolate, and manipulate them. Children who can hear sounds in words have an advantage in that they can connect specific sounds with the letters that represent them.
Letter Knowledge	Letter knowledge refers to what children need to learn about the graphic characters—how they look, how to distinguish one from another, how to detect them within continuous text, how to use them in words. A finite set of twenty-six letters, two forms of each, is related to all of the sounds of the English language (forty-four phonemes). The sounds in the language change as dialect, articulation, and other speech factors vary. Children will also encounter alternative forms of some letters—for example, *a* and *a*—and will eventually learn to recognize letters in cursive writing. Children need to learn the names and purposes of letters, as well as the distinguishing features (the small differences that help them separate a *d* from an *a,* for example). When children can identify letters, they can associate them with sounds, and the alphabetic principle is mastered.
Letter-Sound Relationships	The sounds of oral language are related in both simple and complex ways to the twenty-six letters of the alphabet. Learning the connections between letters and sounds is basic to understanding written language. Children tend to learn the "regular" connections between letters and sounds (*b* for the first sound in *bat*) first. But they also must learn that often letters appear together—for example, it is efficient to think of the two sounds at the beginning of *black* together. Sometimes a single sound (like /ch/) is connected to two letters; sometimes a cluster of letters represents one sound, for example, *eigh* for long *a.* Children learn to look for and recognize these letter combinations as units, which makes their word solving more efficient.
Spelling Patterns	Efficient word solvers look for and find patterns in the way words are constructed. Knowing spelling patterns or word parts helps children notice and use larger parts of words, thus making word solving faster and easier. Patterns are also helpful to children in writing words, because they can quickly write down the patterns rather than laboriously working with individual sounds and letters.
High-Frequency Words	A core of high-frequency words is a valuable resource as children build their reading and writing processing systems. We can also call these *high-utility* words because they appear often and can sometimes be used to help in solving other words. Recognizing high-frequency words automatically frees attention for understanding as well as for solving other new words. In general, children first learn simple high-frequency words and in the process develop efficient systems for learning more words; the process accelerates. They continuously add to the core of high-frequency words they know. Lessons on high-frequency words can develop automaticity and help children look more carefully at the features of words.

FIGURE I-1 *(continued)*

Word Meaning/ Vocabulary	*Vocabulary* refers to the words one knows as part of language. For comprehension and coherence, students need to know the meanings of the words in the texts they read and write. It is important for them to constantly expand their listening, speaking, reading, and writing vocabularies and to develop more complex understandings of words they already know (for example, words may have multiple meanings or be used figuratively).
Word Structure	Words are built according to rules. Looking at the structure of words will help students learn how words are related to each other and how they can be changed by adding letters, letter clusters, and larger word parts. Readers who can break down words into syllables and can notice categories of word parts can apply their word-solving strategies efficiently.
Word-Solving Actions	Word solving is related to all of the categories of learning previously described, but we have created an additional category that focuses on the strategic moves readers and writers make when they use their knowledge of the language system while reading and writing continuous text. These strategies are "in-the-head" actions that are invisible, although we can often infer them from overt behaviors.

help you plan for teaching. You can match up these principles with the curriculum in your school. They also are a match for our *Fountas & Pinnell Phonics, Spelling, and Word Study Lessons,* as well as for the grade-by-grade Phonics, Spelling, and Word Study continuum in *The Fountas & Pinnell Literacy Continuum* (2017).

Early in schooling, and many times before they begin schooling, students learn critical concepts about how print works. There are particular conventions in print that must be brought under control—for example, word-by-word matching and left-to-right directionality. As well, students live in a world of print and soon begin to notice letters and to connect them to the sounds of language. They move from these broad areas to the complexities of the various parts of speech and their functions and to details of word structure. Students learn to take multisyllable words apart and to use prefixes, suffixes, and base words not only to decode words but also to help them derive meaning. They learn to use word roots and historical information to understand word meaning.

Learning over Time

Curriculum plans sometimes give the impression that learning takes place at *one* point in time. Once "taught," it should be learned. That may be true for some single facts, but complex learning takes time over many examples and a great deal of use. Each one of the nine areas requires several years for a student to achieve a high level of learning, one that assures the student is not learning a narrow definition but is developing deep, internalized understanding that allows him to apply the understanding constantly and usually without conscious effort. That means that students are working across each of these areas in a kind of spiraled learning so that understandings in each increase in complexity over time.

Students typically achieve control over the first three areas, Early Literacy Concepts, Phonological Awareness, and Letter Knowledge, by the end of grade one, so those areas drop off the chart. Learning in the next six areas continues over the following years. Students learn in some subcategories more quickly than others. Some areas are so complex that they must be controlled gradually over time, as shown in Figure I-2.

Moreover, the learning is by no means complete after middle school. Most of us continue to learn more about language our whole lives—and we do it through use.

Teaching with Precise Language

After each behavior, we have placed some language to explain the principle that underlies the behavior. It is important to use clear, consistent language with students. Often, you will see several sentences that indicate variations or progressions in learning the principle. (You might need more than one mini-lesson to teach the principle.) It is important not only to use clear, simple language but also to write it on a chart with examples so that it remains visible to children. The goal is to have students internalize the language eventually. The language also keeps us from "talking too much." Of course, this is not a script, and you might want to vary it to meet your students' needs. But once you establish clear language, try to say it the same way every time.

We do advocate explicit phonics and word study lessons that have an element of inquiry; however, we recognize also that it is essential for students to learn how words work through reading and writing continuous text. By itself, a phonics or word study lesson will not help you achieve what you want for your students. They need to use this information *all the time* as they read and write.

Reading

When learners read continuous text, the meaning and the language support their learning about the print. Readers use all of their current understandings to read the words accurately. As they approach a word, they might think:

▶ What would make sense and look right here? *(using meaning in combination with letter-sound and phonological information)*

▶ What would sound right in language and also look right? *(using language syntax in combination with letter-sound and phonological information)*

▶ What would look like this and make sense in this sentence? *(using letter-sound and phonological information along with meaning)*

▶ Does what I just read look right, sound right, and make sense? *(using letter-sound and phonological information, language syntax, and meaning)*

FIGURE I-2 *Areas of Learning*

AREAS OF LEARNING	GRADES IN WHICH STUDENTS ARE WORKING TO ACHIEVE CONTROL OVER LEARNING
1. Early Literacy Concepts	*PreK, K, 1*
2. Phonological Awareness	
a. Rhyming Words	a. *PreK, K, 1*
b. Words	b. *K*
c. Syllables	c. *PreK, K, 1*
d. Onsets and Rimes	d. *K, 1*
e. Phonemes	e. *K, 1*
3. Letter Knowledge	
a. Identifying Letters	a. *PreK, K, 1*
b. Recognizing Letters in Words and Sentences	b. *PreK, K, 1*
c. Forming Letters	c. *K, 1, 2, 3*
4. Letter-Sound Relationships	
a. Consonants	a. *K, 1, 2, 3, 4, 5, 6*
b. Vowels	b. *K, 1, 2, 3, 4*
c. Letter-Sound Representations	c. *1, 2, 3, 4*
5. Spelling Patterns	
a. Phonogram Patterns	a. *PreK, K, 1, 2, 3, 4, 5*
b. Vowel Phonogram Patterns in Single-Syllable Words	b. *1, 2, 3, 4*
c. Assorted Patterns in Multisyllable Words	c. *2, 3, 4, 5*
d. Vowel Phonogram Patterns in Multisyllable Words	d. *3, 4, 5, 6, 7, 8*
6. High-Frequency Words	*K, 1, 2, 3, 4, 5, 6, 7, 8*
7. Word Meaning/Vocabulary	
a. Concept Words	a. *K, 1, 2, 3, 4*
b. Related Words	b. *K, 1, 2, 3, 4, 5, 6, 7, 8*
c. Combined and Created Words	c. *1, 2, 3, 4, 5, 6, 7, 8*
d. Figurative Uses of Words	d. *3, 4, 5, 6, 7, 8*
e. Parts of Words	e. *3, 4, 5, 6, 7, 8*
f. Word Origins	f. *3, 4, 5, 6, 7, 8*

FIGURE I-2 *(continued)*

AREAS OF LEARNING	GRADES IN WHICH STUDENTS ARE WORKING TO ACHIEVE CONTROL OVER LEARNING
8. Word Structure	
a. Syllables	a. *K, 1, 2, 3, 4, 5*
b. Compound Words	b. *1, 2, 3, 4*
c. Contractions	c. *K, 1, 2, 3, 4, 5, 6, 7, 8*
d. Plurals	d. *K, 1, 2, 3, 4, 5, 6, 7, 8*
e. Possessives	e. *1, 2, 3, 4, 5*
f. Suffixes	f. *K, 1, 2, 3, 4, 5, 6, 7, 8*
• Suffixes: Inflectional Endings	
• Suffixes: Comparative Endings	
• Suffixes: Verb Suffixes	
• Suffixes: Adjective and Adverb Suffixes	
• Suffixes: Noun Suffixes	
g. Prefixes	g. *2, 3, 4, 5, 6, 7, 8*
h. Abbreviations	h. *1, 2, 3, 4, 5, 6, 7, 8*
i. Word Roots	i. *4, 5, 6, 7, 8*
9. Word-Solving Actions	
a. Using What Is Known to Solve Words	a. *PreK, 1, 2, 3, 4, 5*
b. Analyzing Words to Solve Them	b. *PreK, 1, 2, 3*
c. Changing, Adding, or Removing Parts to Solve Words	c. *K, 1, 2, 3*
d. Taking Words Apart to Solve Them	d. *1, 2, 3, 4, 5, 6, 7, 8*
e. Using Strategies to Solve Words and Determine Their Meanings	e. *1, 2, 3, 4, 5, 6, 7, 8*
f. Using Reference Tools to Solve and Find Information About Words	f. *1, 2, 3, 4, 5, 6, 7, 8*
g. Spelling Strategies	g. *K, 1, 2, 3, 4, 5, 6, 7, 8*

Readers use several sources of information in a highly flexible way both to solve words and to monitor their reading and self-correct. These behaviors are obvious in beginning readers; more advanced readers do not display as much overt behavior as younger readers, and they are orchestrating far more complex versions of these systems of information. For example, advanced readers determine meaning in words that are part of a wide vocabulary and that are typical of written language, including many words with multiple meanings. Readers use their understanding of complex sentence structure and of nuances of written language that require inference. All of this information supports and works in combination with the sophisticated way students are taking apart multisyllable words. In short, when students are reading continuous text, they have much more information at their disposal. They are rewarded with meaning.

It may not seem obvious, but interactive read-aloud also contributes substantially to students' ability to learn about words. As they listen to texts read aloud, students hear the sounds of language and build a listening vocabulary. When they already know the meaning of a word and can use it orally, it is much more available to them phonetically, visually, and structurally. It means more. Reading aloud to your students daily is a "must" in classroom teaching—not just for learning about words but also for comprehending and enjoying reading.

Shared Reading

Shared reading is a context in which the teacher and children read an enlarged text together. This highly supported situation allows students to process a more complex text than they could do independently. They read the book several times, and on successive re-readings, they have the opportunity to pay more attention to the visual and phonological information. Children can use highlighter tape to identify letters (first or last), significant word parts, or high-frequency words.

Shared reading is used for older students as well, often involving a projected text or individual copies of the same text. Individual copies are frequently used for readers' theater or close analysis, which usually focuses on comprehension. But there are often opportunities for students to notice interesting words and to identify base words, word roots, and affixes.

Guided Reading

Guided reading is small-group instruction. You work with a small group of students who are similar in their development of a reading process, with the goal of learning more about reading. Using assessment data, you bring together groups of individuals who are similar enough that you can involve them in reading the same book that you select. The text is just a little more challenging than students can read independently. You introduce the text and then provide supportive teaching to help students read this more challenging text with proficiency. The structure of guided reading is:

- The teacher selects the text.
- The teacher introduces the text and engages students' interest.
- The students read the text, sometimes with brief interactions with the teacher. Here you can teach, prompt, or reinforce effective reading behaviors, including powerful, strategic word-solving actions.
- The students discuss the text.
- The teacher does some specific teaching designed to help students learn something about processing that they can apply to their reading of other texts.
- The teacher engages students in brief "hands-on" work with words (for example, using magnetic letters or word cards).

Across the guided reading lesson, you can teach for effective word-solving strategies. In the introduction, you can show students something about a few new or important words. While students are reading the text, you can sample oral reading and prompt for effective strategic actions (see *The Fountas & Pinnell Prompting Guide Part 1 for Oral Reading and Early Writing*). After the discussion, you may decide to do some specific teaching about word solving using a word from the text that is particularly challenging or to evoke productive behavior on the part of one of the students. At the end of the guided reading lesson, you can involve students in a few minutes of active work with words. They might sort letters or words, work with magnetic letters, make words, take words apart, and connect words by word part, base word, or word root. The idea here is to be very specific about what students need to know in order to solve words in texts at the particular level where you are teaching.

Writing

Writing makes a powerful contribution to phonics and word understanding. When students write, the process is slowed down: They say words slowly to hear sounds or parts, and they construct the words letter by letter or part by part. Beginning writers can engage in powerful group processes like shared and interactive writing.

Shared Writing

In shared writing, the teacher is the scribe, writing on an easel so all can see. Together, the students and the teacher compose a text for any purpose needed. There are many opportunities for teaching about the construction of words. Students can say words slowly and think about the sounds. They can notice parts of words and make connections between words.

Interactive Writing

An adaptation of shared writing is interactive writing. The only difference here is that, occasionally, when there is instructional value, the teacher invites a student to come up to the easel and write a letter, a word, or a part of a word.

This process gives young students a very personal stake in the writing, and it focuses their attention. The process is always changing. The teacher writes words or parts that are too difficult for children to take on at this time and also writes words that students know well and don't need to attend to.

Usually interactive writing is used only in the early grades or with small groups who need it at other levels. As students grow in proficiency they write a great deal for themselves. Coming up to the easel would be unnecessarily time-consuming and have less instructional value. But you will still use shared writing and can take the opportunity to teach about word structure.

Independent Writing

Students learn a great deal about words through their own independent writing. It is here that they have the opportunity to compose texts and spell words for their own purposes. Just as reading is a breaking-down process, writing is a building-up process. Students learn how to say and listen to sounds and word parts to construct them, and they learn how to notice and use patterns to construct new words. Through examining students' writing over time, you can get good evidence of what they understand about the structure of words.

Phonics, Word Study, and Spelling Lessons

The items in the various sections of this chart are not intended to be a curriculum that is carried only by direct lessons. It is very important for there to be strong connections between your direct and explicit lessons and the application activities in which you engage students in reading and writing. The comprehensive chart can help you

- plan inquiry-based lessons, application activities, and group share;
- remind students of principles in writing minilessons and in conferences about their writing;
- remind students of principles in shared or interactive writing and when you interact with them as they read text; and
- plan for word work at the end of a guided reading lesson (see *Guided Reading: Responsive Teaching Across the Grades, Second Edition,* 2017).

We have described a simple structure for phonics, spelling, and word study instruction. In general, this structure works across the grades, with the principles and examples growing more complex over time, of course. The structure is described in Figure I-3.

Provide an explicit lesson as frequently as possible for younger students and about one or two times a week for intermediate or middle-level students. (Remember that students will also be learning about words in reading and writing.) The phonics program is a lively, interesting look at words and how they work. Your goal is to get your students interested in words—seeking patterns, looking for connections, thinking about the parts and what they mean.

FIGURE I-3 *Structure for Phonics, Spelling, and Word Study*

Phonics, Spelling, and Word Study Lesson	The teacher provides a concise lesson based on one clear principle related to any point on the chart.	• Often the teacher asks students to study some examples of words that exemplify the principle. • The students describe the principle. • The teacher writes it in precise language on a chart or easel. • The students generate more examples. • The teacher explains the application activity.
Application	Students engage in an active, "hands-on" application activity independently or with a partner.	• The application activity is based on routines that students have been taught and that they know well. • They might sort letters, make words, sort words, write, or engage in other active exploration that offers opportunities for students to make their own discoveries. • Students can work with a partner for interactional support.
Group Share	Students meet for a brief discussion at the end of the period.	• Students can share what they discovered through application. • The teacher returns to the lesson principle, using clear language that students can remember.

Efficient Word Solving—the Goal of Phonics and Word Study Instruction

As readers and writers build their word-solving competencies, they develop a repertoire for solving words that they use in powerful and flexible ways. You help them to be as efficient as possible in the process, knowing that the more attention they have to give to word solving, the less attention they will have for comprehending texts. Connecting sounds to larger units in words makes word solving more efficient. Kaye's study of proficient second-grade readers (2008) indicated that they had more than sixty ways to solve words and tended to work with larger word units rather than "sounding out" a word letter by letter (although they could).

Readers who can use phonogram patterns to connect isolated words also need to notice such patterns in words they read (or have read to them) within continuous text; they can use these patterns to solve one- and two-syllable words. As the demands of texts increase over the upper elementary grades, students have the opportunity to apply knowledge of patterns to much longer words. In addition to phonogram patterns, they use knowledge of consonant blends and digraphs as well as double letters and silent letters. Spelling patterns including vowel combinations (such as *-ail* and *-ain*), for example, appear frequently in both single-syllable and multisyllable words. Patterns such as *-alk*,

-aught, -ought, and *-ong,* as well as *-oon, -ew, -ue,* and *-ule,* pose challenges in both reading and spelling.

Using the Comprehensive Guide

We have described ways you can use this comprehensive guide both for explicit lessons and across contexts for reading and writing. As you use it, these organizational features will help:

▶ division into nine areas of learning, bringing together extensive information and knowledge in the form of strategic word-solving actions;

▶ subdivision of areas of learning into categories;

▶ a list of specific behaviors and principles for each category;

▶ instructional (child-friendly) language for each principle;

▶ distribution of learning across the grade levels for each behavior and principle—indicated by dots on the chart, and including demarcations of early, middle, and late in the school year (indicated by *E, M,* and *L* in the right columns of the chart); and

▶ a glossary providing definitions of linguistic terms.

This chart is a reference for you. As proficient adult readers and writers, it is impossible for us to keep all of this information in mind all the time (and we don't need to). But in teaching, it is helpful to have a comprehensive reference tool to undergird our teaching. We hope you find it so!

Early Literacy Concepts

Early Literacy Concepts

Learning about literacy begins long before children enter school. Many children hear stories read aloud and try out writing for themselves; through such experiences, they learn some basic concepts about written language. Nearly all children begin to notice print in the environment and develop ideas about the purposes of print. The child's name, for example, is a very important word. Kindergartners and first graders are still acquiring some of these basic concepts, and they need to generalize and systematize their knowledge. In the classroom, they learn a great deal through experiences like shared and modeled reading and shared and interactive writing. Explicit teaching can help children learn much more about these early concepts, understand their importance, and develop ways of using them in reading and writing.

EARLY LITERACY CONCEPTS

	BEHAVIOR	INSTRUCTIONAL LANGUAGE	PreK E	PreK M	PreK L	K E	K M	K L	1 E	1 M	1 L	2 E	2 M	2 L	3 E	3 M	3 L	4 E	4 M	4 L	5 E	5 M	5 L	6	7	8
1	Distinguish and talk about the differences between pictures and print.	The pictures can be drawings, paintings, or photographs. The print is the words on a page. The pictures and the print are two ways writers give information. The pictures and the print are both important.	●	●	●	●																				
2	Understand and talk about the purpose of print in reading.	The print is the words on a page. The print tells a story or gives other information. Read the print to understand stories and messages.	●	●	●	●																				
3	Understand and talk about the purpose of print in writing.	The print is the words on a page. The print tells a story or gives other information. Writers use letters and words to tell stories and give information.	●	●	●	●																				
4	Understand and talk about the concept of a letter.	A letter has a shape and a name.	●	●	●	●	●	●	●	●																
5	Understand and talk about the concept of a word.	A word has one or more letters with a space on each side of the word. A word means something.				●	●	●	●	●																
6	Recognize and point to one's name.	A name is a word. When you know the first letter in a name, it helps you find the name in print. A name starts with a capital letter. The other letters are lowercase.	●	●	●	●																				
7	Use left-to-right directionality of print.	Read and write from left to right.	●	●	●	●																				
8	Use letters from one's name to represent it or to write a message.	Write the letters in your name. Use the letters in your name along with other letters to write messages.	●	●	●	●	●																			

E = Early in school year, M = Mid-year, L = Late in school year

EARLY LITERACY CONCEPTS (continued)

	BEHAVIOR	INSTRUCTIONAL LANGUAGE	PreK			K			1			2			3			4			5			6–8		
			E	M	L	E	M	L	E	M	L	E	M	L	E	M	L	E	M	L	E	M	L	6	7	8
9	Understand and talk about the concepts of first and last in written language.	The first letter in a word is on the left. The last letter in a word is on the right. The first word in a sentence is on the left. There are spaces between the words in a sentence. The last word in a sentence is before the period or question mark or exclamation mark. The first part of a page is at the top. The last part of a page is at the bottom.	●	●	●	●	●	●																			
10	Understand and demonstrate that one spoken word matches one group of letters.	Say one word for each group of letters.	●	●	●	●	●	●																			
11	Use one's name to learn about words and to make connections to words.	A name is a word. Connect your name with other words.	●	●	●	●	●	●	●																		
12	Locate the first and last letters of words in continuous text.	Find a word by noticing how it looks. Find a word by looking for the first letter. Check a word by looking at the first and last letters.						●	●	●	●																
13	Understand and talk about the concept of a sentence.	A sentence is a group of words that makes sense.										●	●	●													
14	Understand and talk about the concept of a book.	A book has a front cover, pages, and a back cover. A book has a title and an author. A book often has pictures. Hold a book on the two sides with the top of the book above and the bottom of the book below. Turn the pages of a book to read the print from the front of the book to the back of the book. A book has information in it.	●	●	●	●	●	●	●																		

Phonological Awareness

Phonological Awareness

Phonological awareness refers to both explicit and implicit knowledge of the sounds in language. It includes the ability to identify and make rhymes, hear syllables in words, hear the parts of words (onsets and rimes), and hear individual sounds in words. *Phonemic awareness* is one kind of phonological awareness. It refers to the ability to identify, isolate, and manipulate the individual sounds (phonemes) in words. Principles categorized as phonemic awareness appear under the heading Phonemes.

Phonological awareness can be taught orally. When it is taught in connection with letters, it is called *phonics*. Phonics instruction refers to teaching children to connect sounds and letters in words. While very early experiences focus on hearing and saying sounds in the absence of letters, most of the time you will want to teach children to hear sounds in connection with letters. Many classroom lessons related to the principles below could begin with teaching orally but move toward connecting the sounds to letters. You will not want to teach all of the principles under Phonemes. It is more effective to teach children only two or three ways to manipulate phonemes in words so that they learn how words work.

Principles related to letter-sound relationships, or phonics, are included in the Letter-Sound Relationships area of learning.

PHONOLOGICAL AWARENESS																										
BEHAVIOR	**INSTRUCTIONAL LANGUAGE**	GRADE LEVEL																								
		PreK			K			1			2			3			4			5			6-8		
		E	M	L	E	M	L	E	M	L	E	M	L	E	M	L	E	M	L	E	M	L	6	7	8
Rhyming Words																										
1 Hear and say rhyming words: e.g., *new, blue.*	Some words have parts at the end that sound the same. They rhyme. Listen for the rhymes in poems and songs. Say words and listen for how they rhyme.	•	•	•	•	•	•	•	•																	
2 Hear and connect rhyming words: e.g., *fly, high, buy, sky.*	Listen for and connect words that rhyme.	•	•	•	•	•	•	•	•																	
3 Hear and generate rhyming words: e.g., *a bug in a ___ (hug, jug, mug, rug).*	Make rhymes by playing with words and thinking of words that sound the same at the end.	•	•	•	•	•	•	•	•																	
Words																										
4 Hear and recognize word boundaries.	Say each word when you are talking. Say each word in a sentence by stopping after each one.					•	•	•																		
5 Divide sentences into words: e.g., *I - like - to - play.*	Say each word in a sentence.					•	•	•																		

BEHAVIOR	INSTRUCTIONAL LANGUAGE	PreK			K			1			2			3			4			5			6-8		
		E	M	L	E	M	L	E	M	L	E	M	L	E	M	L	E	M	L	E	M	L	6	7	8
Syllables																									
6 Hear, say, and clap syllables: e.g., *farm, be/fore, a/ni/mal.*	Words can have one or more parts. Listen for, say, and clap the parts in a word.			●	●	●	●	●	●	●															
7 Blend syllables: e.g., *let/ter, letter.*	Blend the parts in a word.				●	●	●	●	●	●															
8 Divide words into syllables: e.g., *never, nev/er.*	Break a word into parts.				●	●	●	●	●	●															
9 Delete a syllable from a word: e.g., *a/round, round; be/hind, be.*	Remove a part from some words to make a new word.				●	●	●	●	●	●															
Onsets and Rimes																									
10 Hear and divide onsets and rimes: e.g., *m-en, bl-ack.*	Listen for and say the first and last parts of a word.							●	●	●	●														
11 Blend onsets with rimes: e.g., *d-og, dog.*	Blend the parts of a word.							●	●	●	●														
Phonemes																									
12 Hear and say two phonemes (sounds) in a word: e.g., */a/ /t/.*	Say a word slowly. Listen for each sound in a word.						●	●	●	●															
13 Divide a word into phonemes: e.g., *no, /n/ /ō/.*	Say each sound in a word.						●	●	●	●															
14 Hear and say three phonemes in a word: e.g., */r/ /u/ /n/.*	Say a word slowly. Listen for each sound in a word.						●	●	●	●															
15 Hear and say the beginning phoneme in a word: e.g., *sun, /s/.*	Say a word to hear the first sound. Listen for the first sound in a word.						●	●	●	●	●														
16 Hear and say the ending phoneme in a word: e.g., *bed, /d/.*	Say a word to hear the last sound. Listen for the last sound in a word.						●	●	●	●	●														
17 Hear and say the same beginning phoneme in words: e.g., *run, red, /r/.*	Some words sound the same at the beginning. Connect words that sound the same at the beginning.						●	●	●	●	●														
18 Hear and say the same ending phoneme in words: e.g., *win, fun, /n/.*	Some words sound the same at the end. Connect words that sound the same at the end.						●	●	●	●	●														
19 Blend two or three phonemes in a word: e.g., */l/ /o/ /t/, lot.*	Blend the sounds to say a word.							●	●	●	●														
20 Add a phoneme to the beginning of a word: e.g., */s/ + it = sit.*	Add a sound to the beginning of a word to make a new word.							●	●	●	●	●													

PHONOLOGICAL AWARENESS

PHONOLOGICAL AWARENESS *(continued)*

BEHAVIOR	INSTRUCTIONAL LANGUAGE	PreK			K			1			2			3			4			5			6–8		
		E	M	L	E	M	L	E	M	L	E	M	L	E	M	L	E	M	L	E	M	L	6	7	8
Phonemes *(continued)*																									
21 Change the beginning phoneme to make a new word: e.g., *not, hot* (change /n/ to /h/).	Change the first sound in a word to make a new word.					•	•	•	•	•															
22 Change the ending phoneme to make a new word: e.g., *his, him,* (change /s/ to /m/).	Change the last sound in a word to make a new word.					•	•	•	•	•															
23 Hear and say the middle phoneme in a word with three phonemes: e.g., *fit,* /i/.	Listen for and say the sound in the middle of a word.					•	•	•	•	•															
24 Hear and say the same middle phoneme in words: e.g., *cat, ran,* /a/.	Some words sound the same in the middle. Connect words that sound the same in the middle.					•	•	•	•	•															
25 Hear and say four or more phonemes in a word in sequence: e.g., /s/ /p/ /e/ /n/ /d/.	Say a word slowly. Listen for each sound in a word.							•	•	•	•														
26 Blend three or four phonemes in a word: e.g., /n/ /e/ /s/ /t/, *nest.*	Blend the sounds to say a word.							•	•	•	•														
27 Delete the beginning phoneme of a word: e.g., *can, an* (delete /k/).	Say a word without the first sound.							•	•	•	•														
28 Delete the ending phoneme of a word: e.g., *wind, win* (delete /d/).	Say a word without the last sound.							•	•	•	•														
29 Add a phoneme to the end of a word: e.g., *an* + /d/ = *and.*	Add a sound to the end of a word to make a new word.							•	•	•	•														
30 Change the middle phoneme in a word with three phonemes to make a new word: e.g., *hit, hat,* (change /i/ to /a/).	Change a sound in the middle of a word to make a new word.							•	•	•	•														

Letter Knowledge

Letter Knowledge

Letter knowledge refers to what children need to learn about the graphic characters that correspond with the sounds of language. A finite set of twenty-six letters, two forms of each, is related to all of the sounds of the English language (approximately forty-four phonemes). The sounds in the language change as dialect, articulation, and other speech factors vary. Children will also encounter alternative forms of some letters—for example, g, g; ɑ, a; t, t—and will eventually learn to recognize letters in cursive writing. Children need to learn the purpose and function of letters, as well as the name and particular features of each one. When children can identify letters by noticing the very small differences that make them unique, they can then associate letters and letter clusters with phonemes and parts of words. Knowing the letter names is useful information that helps children talk about letters and understand what others say about them. As writers, children need to be able to use efficient directional movements when making letters.

LETTER KNOWLEDGE

BEHAVIOR	INSTRUCTIONAL LANGUAGE	PreK E	PreK M	PreK L	K E	K M	K L	1 E	1 M	1 L	2 E	2 M	2 L	3 E	3 M	3 L	4 E	4 M	4 L	5 E	5 M	5 L	6	7	8
Identifying Letters																									
1 Recognize and point to the distinctive features of letter forms.	Each letter looks different. Some letters have long straight lines. Some letters have short straight lines. Some letters have curves [e.g., circles, tails].	•	•	•	•	•	•	•																	
2 Recognize letters and state their names.	Look at the shape of a letter and say its name.	•	•	•	•	•	•	•																	
3 Recognize and point to uppercase letters and lowercase letters: e.g., *B, b.*	There are two kinds of letters. One is uppercase (or capital), and the other is lowercase (or small).							•	•	•															
4 Distinguish and talk about the differences between the uppercase and lowercase forms of a letter.	Some uppercase letters and lowercase letters look the same [e.g., W, w]. Some uppercase letters and lowercase letters look different [e.g., R, r]. A name starts with an uppercase letter. The other letters in a name are lowercase letters.							•	•	•															
5 Categorize letters by features.	Some letters have parts that look the same. Some letters have long straight lines [e.g., d, p]. Some letters have short straight lines [e.g., i, n]. Some letters have curves [e.g., e, c]. Some letters have dots [e.g., i, j]. Some letters have tunnels [e.g., h, n].							•	•	•	•														
6 Recognize and talk about the order of the alphabet.	The alphabet has twenty-six letters. The letters are in a special order.							•	•	•	•														

		BEHAVIOR	INSTRUCTIONAL LANGUAGE	GRADE LEVEL																								
				PreK			K			1			2			3			4			5			6–8		
				E	M	L	E	M	L	E	M	L	E	M	L	E	M	L	E	M	L	E	M	L	6	7	8
Identifying Letters *(continued)*																												
7		Recognize and talk about the fact that letters can be consonants or vowels.	*Some letters are consonants: b, c, d, f, g, h, j, k, l, m, n, p, q, r, s, t, v, w, x, y, z.* *Some letters are vowels: a, e, i, o, u, and sometimes y.* *Every word has at least one vowel.*						●	●	●	●																	
Recognizing Letters in Words and Sentences																												
8		Recognize and name letters in the environment (signs, labels, etc.).	*Letters or words appear on signs, labels, and other objects.* *Say the names of letters or say words printed on objects.*	●	●	●	●	●	●																			
9		Understand and talk about the fact that words are formed with letters.	*Put letters together to make a word.* *Your name is a word.* *Put letters together to make your name.* *Say the letters in your name.*	●	●	●	●	●	●	●																		
10		Recognize and name letters in words.	*Find letters in words.* *Say the names of letters in words.*	●	●	●	●	●	●	●	●																	
11		Recognize and talk about the sequence of letters in a word.	*The letters in a word are always in the same order.* *The first letter is on the left.* *Find and name the first letter in a word.* *Find and name all of the letters in a word in order.*				●	●	●	●	●																	
12		Recognize and name letters in words in continuous text.	*Find letters in words in sentences.*				●	●	●	●	●																	
13		Make connections among words by recognizing the position of a letter: e.g., _wa_s, _we_; goo_d_, sai_d_; ju_st_, p_ut_.	*Find words that begin with the same letter.* *Find words that end with the same letter.* *Find words that have the same letter in the middle.*				●	●	●	●	●																	
Forming Letters																												
14		Use efficient and consistent motions to form letters in manuscript print with writing tools.	*Make the shape of a letter.* *Say the steps you use to make a letter.* *Check to see if a letter looks right.*				●	●	●	●	●	●	●	●	●													
15		Use efficient and consistent motions to form letters in cursive writing with writing tools.	*Make the shape of a letter in cursive writing.* *Say the steps you use to make a letter in cursive writing.* *Check to see if a letter looks right.*													●	●	●										

Letter-Sound Relationships

Letter-Sound Relationships

The sounds of oral language are related in both simple and complex ways to the twenty-six letters of the alphabet. Learning the connections between letters and sounds is basic to understanding written language. You will want to connect initial sounds to letters using the Alphabet Linking Chart to support early understandings and the Consonant Cluster Linking Chart as they learn more. Children first learn simple relationships that are regular in that one phoneme is connected to one grapheme, or letter. But sounds are also connected to letter clusters, which are groups of letters that appear often together (for example, *cr, str, st, bl, fr*), in which you hear the sound associated with each of the letters; and consonant digraphs (*sh, ch*), in which you hear a sound that is different from the sound of either consonant. Vowels may also appear in combinations in which usually you hear the sound of the first vowel only (*ai, ea, oa*) or in which you hear a sound that is different from the sound of either vowel (*ou*). For efficient word solving students need to learn to look for and recognize these letter combinations as units.

LETTER-SOUND RELATIONSHIPS

	BEHAVIOR	INSTRUCTIONAL LANGUAGE	PreK E	PreK M	PreK L	K E	K M	K L	1 E	1 M	1 L	2 E	2 M	2 L	3 E	3 M	3 L	4 E	4 M	4 L	5 E	5 M	5 L	6	7	8
Consonants																										
1	Understand and talk about the fact that some letters represent consonant sounds: e.g., the letter *b* stands for the first sound in *boy*.	Match letters and sounds in a word. / Some letters are consonants.					●	●	●	●	●															
2	Recognize and use beginning consonant sounds and the letters that represent them: *b, c, d, f, g, h, j, k, l, m, n, p, qu, r, s, t, v, w, y, z*.	Say a word slowly and listen for the first sound. / Match sounds and letters at the beginning of a word. / When you know the sound, you can find the letter. The letter q is almost always followed by the letter u. / Find a word by saying it and thinking about the first sound. / When you see a letter at the beginning of a word, you can say the sound it stands for.					●	●	●	●	●															
3	Recognize, point to, and say the same beginning consonant sound and the letter that represents the sound: e.g., <u>b</u>ag, <u>b</u>ee.	Two words can start with the same letter and sound.					●	●	●	●	●															

The Fountas & Pinnell Comprehensive Phonics, Spelling, and Word Study Guide

LETTER-SOUND RELATIONSHIPS (continued)

BEHAVIOR	INSTRUCTIONAL LANGUAGE	PreK			K			1			2			3			4			5			6–8		
		E	M	L	E	M	L	E	M	L	E	M	L	E	M	L	E	M	L	E	M	L	6	7	8
Consonants (continued)																									
4 Recognize and use ending consonant sounds and the letters that represent them: *b, d, f, g, k, l, m, n, p, r, s, t, v, z.*	Listen for the sound at the end of a word. Match sounds and letters at the end of a word. When you know the sound, you can find the letter or letters. Find a word by saying it and thinking about the last sound. When you see a letter at the end of a word, you can say the sound it stands for.							●	●	●	●	●	●	●											
5 Recognize and use medial consonant sounds and the letters that represent them: *b, c, d, e, f, g, h, j, k, l, m, n, p, qu, r, s, t, v, w, x, y, z.*	Listen for the sound or sounds in the middle of a word. Match sounds and letters in the middle of a word. When you know the sound, you can find the letter. The letter q is almost always followed by the letter u. Find a word by saying it and thinking about the sound or sounds in the middle. When you see a letter in the middle of a word, you can say its sound.										●	●	●	●	●	●									
6 Recognize and use ending consonant sounds sometimes represented by double consonant letters: *o<u>ff</u>, hi<u>ll</u>, dre<u>ss</u>, bu<u>zz</u>.*	Sometimes double consonant letters stand for a consonant sound at the end of a word.										●	●	●	●	●										
7 Recognize and say consonant clusters that blend two or three consonant sounds (onsets): *bl, cl, fl, gl, pl, sl, br, cr, dr, fr, gr, pr, tr, sc, sk, sm, sn, sp, st, sw, tw, qu; scr, spl, spr, squ, str.*	A group of two or three consonant letters is a consonant cluster. You can usually hear each sound in a consonant cluster.										●	●	●	●	●	●	●	●							
8 Recognize and use two consonant letters that represent one sound at the beginning of a word: e.g., *<u>ch</u>ange, <u>ph</u>one, <u>sh</u>all, <u>th</u>irty, <u>wh</u>ere.*	Some clusters of consonant letters stand for one sound that is usually different from either of the individual consonant sounds. They are consonant digraphs. You can hear the sound of a consonant digraph at the beginning of a word.									●	●	●	●	●	●	●	●	●							
9 Recognize and use two consonant letters that usually represent one sound at the end of a word: e.g., *bran<u>ch</u>, ro<u>ck</u>, so<u>ng</u>, da<u>sh</u>, bo<u>th</u>.*	Some clusters of consonant letters stand for one sound that is usually different from either of the individual consonant sounds. They are consonant digraphs. You can hear the sound of a consonant digraph at the end of a word.										●	●	●	●	●	●	●	●	●						
10 Recognize and use two consonant letters that represent one sound in the middle of a word: e.g., *ex<u>ch</u>ange, ne<u>ph</u>ew, fi<u>sh</u>es, some<u>th</u>ing, every<u>wh</u>ere, si<u>ng</u>er.*	Some clusters of consonant letters stand for one sound that is usually different from either of the individual consonant sounds. They are consonant digraphs. You can hear the sound of a consonant digraph in the middle of a word.													●	●	●	●	●	●	●	●	●			

LETTER-SOUND RELATIONSHIPS (continued)

BEHAVIOR	INSTRUCTIONAL LANGUAGE	PreK			K			1			2			3			4			5			6-8		
		E	M	L	E	M	L	E	M	L	E	M	L	E	M	L	E	M	L	E	M	L	6	7	8
Consonants *(continued)*																									
11 Recognize and use middle consonant sounds sometimes represented by double consonant letters: *rubber, according, puddle, coffee, bigger, collect, swimmer, announce, dropped, arrive, lesson, attic, buzzing.*	Sometimes double consonant letters stand for one consonant sound in the middle of a word.										•	•	•	•	•	•	•	•	•						
12 Recognize and use consonant letters that represent two or more different sounds at the beginning of a word: *car, city; get, gym; think, they; chair, chorus, choir, chef.*	Some consonants or consonant clusters stand for two or more sounds at the beginning of a word.										•	•	•	•	•	•	•	•	•	•	•	•			
13 Recognize and use consonant letters that represent two or more different sounds at the end of a word: *clinic, spice; hug, cage; rich, stomach; bath, smooth.*	Some consonants or consonant clusters stand for two or more sounds at the end of a word.										•	•	•	•	•	•	•	•	•	•	•	•			
14 Recognize and use consonant letters that represent two or more different sounds in the middle of a word: *cyclone, nicest; bugle, magic; inches, school, machine; mouthwash, feather.*	Some consonants or consonant clusters stand for two or more sounds in the middle of a word.												•	•	•	•	•	•	•	•	•	•	•		
15 Recognize and use consonant clusters (blends) at the end of a word: *ct, ft, ld, lf, lp, lt, mp, nd, nk, nt, pt, sk, sp, st.*	Some words end with a consonant cluster. You can hear each sound in a consonant cluster at the end of a word.										•	•	•	•	•	•	•	•							
16 Recognize and use less frequent consonant digraphs at the beginning or end of a word: *gh, ph* (e.g., *rough, phone, telegraph*).	Consonant digraphs stand for one sound that is different from the sound of either of the consonant letters.													•	•	•	•	•	•	•	•				
17 Recognize and use consonant letters that represent no sound: *lamb, scene, sign, rhyme, know, calm, island, listen, wrap.*	Some words have consonant letters that are silent.													•	•	•	•	•	•	•	•	•			
18 Understand and talk about the fact that some consonant sounds can be represented by several different letters or letter clusters: e.g., *kayak, picnic, truck, stomach, antique; thief, stiff, cough, graph.*	Some consonant sounds are represented by several letters or letter clusters.													•	•	•	•	•	•	•	•	•	•		
Vowels																									
19 Understand and talk about the fact that some letters represent vowel sounds.	Some letters are vowels. Every word has at least one vowel sound. A, e, i, o, and u are vowels (and sometimes y).					•	•	•																	

The Fountas & Pinnell Comprehensive Phonics, Spelling, and Word Study Guide

LETTER-SOUND RELATIONSHIPS (continued)

#	BEHAVIOR	INSTRUCTIONAL LANGUAGE	PreK E	PreK M	PreK L	K E	K M	K L	1 E	1 M	1 L	2 E	2 M	2 L	3 E	3 M	3 L	4 E	4 M	4 L	5 E	5 M	5 L	6	7	8
Vowels (continued)																										
20	Hear and identify short vowel sounds in words and the letters that represent them.	In some words, the letter a stands for the sound you hear at the beginning of apple or the middle of can. In some words, the letter e stands for the sound you hear at the beginning of egg or the middle of get. In some words, the letter i stands for the sound you hear at the beginning of in or the middle of sit. In some words, the letter o stands for the sound you hear at the beginning of on or the middle of hot. In some words, the letter u stands for the sound you hear at the beginning of up or the middle of run.							●	●	●	●														
21	Recognize and use short vowel sounds at the beginning of words: e.g., *at, every, into, onto, up.*	Some words have one vowel at the beginning. The sound of the vowel is short.							●	●	●	●														
22	Recognize and use short vowel sounds in the middle of words (CVC): e.g., *hat, bed, wind, stop, run.*	Some words have one vowel between two consonants. The sound of the vowel is short.							●	●	●	●														
23	Hear and identify long vowel sounds in words and the letters that represent them.	Some words have a long a vowel sound as in lake and paint. Some words have a long e vowel sound as in eat and tree. Some words have a long i vowel sound as in ice and right. Some words have a long o vowel sound as in go and oak. Some words have a long u vowel sound as in use and true.							●	●	●	●	●													
24	Recognize and use long vowel sounds in words with silent *e* (CVCe): e.g., *late, Pete, pine, robe, cube.*	Some words end in an e that is silent, and the other vowel usually has a long sound (sounds like its name).								●	●	●	●	●												
25	Contrast short and long vowel sounds in words: e.g., *at/ate, pet/Pete, bit/bite, hop/hope, cut/cute.*	A vowel can stand for a sound that is different from its name. It is a short vowel sound. A vowel can stand for a sound like its name. It is a long vowel sound.									●	●	●	●	●											

LETTER-SOUND RELATIONSHIPS (continued)

	BEHAVIOR	INSTRUCTIONAL LANGUAGE	PreK E	PreK M	PreK L	K E	K M	K L	1 E	1 M	1 L	2 E	2 M	2 L	3 E	3 M	3 L	4 E	4 M	4 L	5 E	5 M	5 L	6-8 6	6-8 7	6-8 8
	Vowels (continued)																									
26	Recognize and use y as a vowel sound: e.g., *happy, sky.*	Y is a letter that sometimes stands for a vowel sound. Y can stand for a long e vowel sound as in words such as family, funny, happy. Y can stand for a long i vowel sound as in words such as by, my, sky.										•	•	•	•	•	•									
27	Recognize and use letter combinations that represent long vowel sounds: e.g., *chain, play, neat, meet, pie, light, roast, toe, row, blue, fruit, new.*	In some words, two vowels together stand for one sound. When there are two vowels, they usually stand for the sound of the name of the first vowel. In some words, one or more vowels together with one or more consonants can stand for one vowel sound.											•	•	•	•	•	•	•							
28	Recognize and use letter combinations that represent unique vowel sounds: *oi* as in *oil; oy* as in *boy; ou* as in *house; ow* as in *cow.*	Some letters together stand for unique vowel sounds.											•	•	•	•	•	•	•							
29	Recognize and use a letter or letter combinations that represent the /ȯ/ vowel sound (as in *saw*): e.g., *autumn, paw, soft, taught, bought, talk.*	Some letters together stand for the vowel sound heard in saw.											•	•	•	•	•	•	•	•						
30	Recognize and use letter combinations that represent two different vowel sounds: e.g., *meat, break; neighbor, either, height; they key; tie, piece; spoon, book; snow, cow.*	Two letters together can stand for different vowel sounds in different words.													•	•	•	•	•	•						
31	Recognize and use vowel sounds with r: e.g., *chair, care, pear; car; year, pioneer; here; her, first, hurt, learn; corn, more, floor, roar, pour; cure.*	When the letter r follows a vowel or vowel combination, blend the vowel sound with r.													•	•	•	•	•	•						
32	Recognize and use vowel sounds in closed syllables (CVC): *hab/it, lem/on, fig/ure, rob/in, pub/lic.*	Some syllables end with a consonant, and the vowel sound is usually short.											•	•	•	•	•	•	•							
33	Recognize and use vowel sounds in open syllables (CVC): *ba/by, e/ven, pi/lot, ho/tel, hu/man.*	Some syllables end with a vowel, and the vowel sound is usually long.											•	•	•	•	•	•	•							

LETTER-SOUND RELATIONSHIPS (continued)

BEHAVIOR	INSTRUCTIONAL LANGUAGE	PreK			K			1			2			3			4			5			6-8		
		E	M	L	E	M	L	E	M	L	E	M	L	E	M	L	E	M	L	E	M	L	6	7	8

Letter-Sound Representations

	BEHAVIOR	INSTRUCTIONAL LANGUAGE	PreK E	PreK M	PreK L	K E	K M	K L	1 E	1 M	1 L	2 E	2 M	2 L	3 E	3 M	3 L	4 E	4 M	4 L	5 E	5 M	5 L	6	7	8
34	Understand and talk about how to use the computer keyboard.	Use efficient finger movements to type words on a computer keyboard.								•	•	•	•	•	•	•	•	•	•	•	•						
35	Understand and talk about how to use capital letters correctly.	A capital letter at the beginning of the first word shows the beginning of a sentence.							•	•	•	•	•	•	•	•	•	•	•	•	•						
		Capital letters at the beginning of some words show the names of specific people, places, and events.																									
		Use a capital letter for the pronoun I.																									
		Use a capital letter at the beginning of the first word in a direct quotation.																									
		Use capital letters at the beginning of the first word and all important words in the title of a book, magazine article, play, movie, etc.																									
		Use capital letters at the beginning of titles of respect.																									
		Use capital letters at the beginning of the names of races, languages, and religions.																									
		Use capital letters at the beginning of the first word and all important words in the names of businesses and organizations.																									
		Use capital letters at the beginning of some abbreviations and acronyms.																									
36	Understand and talk about how to form cursive letters correctly, efficiently, and fluently.	Write letters smoothly and efficiently in cursive form.														•	•	•	•	•	•						

Spelling Patterns

Spelling Patterns

One way to look at spelling patterns is to examine the way simple words and syllables are put together. Here we include the consonant-vowel-consonant (CVC) pattern in which the vowel often has a short, or terse, sound; the consonant-vowel-consonant-silent *e* (CVC*e*) pattern in which the vowel usually has a long, or lax, sound; and the consonant-vowel-vowel-consonant (CVVC) pattern in which the vowel combination may have either one or two sounds.

Phonograms are spelling patterns that represent the sounds of rimes (last parts of words). They are sometimes called *word families*. You will not need to teach children the technical word *phonogram*, although you may want to use *pattern* or *word part*. A phonogram is the same as a rime, or vowel-bearing part of a word or syllable. We have included a large list of phonograms that will be useful to children in reading or writing, but you will not need to teach every phonogram separately. Once children understand that there are patterns and learn how to look for patterns, they will quickly discover more for themselves.

Knowing spelling patterns helps children notice and use larger parts of words, thus making word solving faster and more efficient. Patterns are also helpful to children in writing words because they will quickly write down the patterns rather than laboriously work with individual sounds and letters. Finally, by knowing to look for patterns and remembering them, children can find connections between words that make word solving easier. In the Behavior column we list a wide range of phonograms. The fourteen most common phonograms are marked with an asterisk in principles 8 and 9.

				SPELLING PATTERNS																						
	BEHAVIOR	**INSTRUCTIONAL LANGUAGE**	**GRADE LEVEL**																							
			PreK			K			1			2			3			4			5			6-8		
			E	M	L	E	M	L	E	M	L	E	M	L	E	M	L	E	M	L	E	M	L	6	7	8
Phonogram Patterns																										
1	Recognize and talk about the fact that words, in general, have letter patterns that can appear in many words.	Some words have parts or patterns that are the same. Notice parts or patterns that are the same in many words.	●	●	●	●	●	●	●	●	●	●															
2	Recognize and use the consonant-vowel-consonant (CVC) pattern: e.g., *cap, get, pig, got, but.*	Some words have a consonant, a vowel, and then another consonant. The vowel sounds like the a in apple, the e in egg, the i in in, the o in octopus, or the u in umbrella.					●	●	●	●	●	●															
3	Recognize and use more common phonograms with a VC pattern: -ab, -ad, -ag, -am, -an, -ap, -at, -aw, -ay; -ed, -en, -et, -ew; -id, -ig, -im, -in, -ip, -it; -ob, -od, -og, -op, -ot, -ow (as in *show* or as in *cow*); -ub, -ug, -um, -un, -ut.	Look at a part or pattern to read a word. Use the part or pattern to write a word. Make new words by putting a letter or a letter cluster before the part or pattern.							●	●	●	●	●	●	●												
4	Recognize and use less common phonograms with a VC pattern: -ax; -eg, -em, -ep, -ex, -ey; -ib, -ix; -on, -ox, -oy; -ud, -up, -us.	Look at the spelling pattern to read a word. Use the spelling pattern to write a word. Make new words by putting a letter or a letter cluster before the pattern.										●	●	●	●	●	●										

SPELLING PATTERNS (continued)

BEHAVIOR	INSTRUCTIONAL LANGUAGE	PreK			K			1			2			3			4			5			6-8		
		E	M	L	E	M	L	E	M	L	E	M	L	E	M	L	E	M	L	E	M	L	6	7	8
Phonogram Patterns (continued)																									
5 Recognize and use phonograms with a vowel-consonant-silent e (VCe) pattern: -ace, -ade, -ake, -ale, -ame, -ane, -ape, -ate, -ave; -ice, -ide, -ile, -ine, -ite, -ive; -oke, -ose.	Some words have a vowel, a consonant, and silent e. The vowel sound is usually the name of the first vowel [the a in place, i in ripe, o in rode, u in tube].					•	•	•	•	•	•	•	•	•											
6 Recognize and use phonograms that end with a double consonant (VCC): e.g., -all, -ass; -ell, -ess; -ill; -uff.	Some words have a double consonant at the end. The sound of the vowel is usually short [the a in class, the e in bell, the i in hill, the u in puff].									•	•	•	•	•	•										
7 Recognize and use phonograms with a double vowel (VVC): -eed, -eek, -eel, -eem, -een, -eep, -eer, -eet; -ood, -oof, -ook, -ool, -oom, -oon, -oop, -oor, -oot.	Some words have a double vowel followed by a consonant. Sometimes a double vowel sounds like the name of the vowel (long sound) [e.g., ee in feed, ee in seem]. Sometimes a double vowel stands for other vowel sounds [e.g., oo in good, oo in room].									•	•	•	•	•	•										
8 Recognize and use phonograms with ending consonant clusters (VCC): e.g., ack*, -act, -aft, -amp, -and, -ang, -ank*, -ant, -ash*, -ask, -ast, -ath; -eck, -elt, -end, -ent, -ept, -est*; -ick*, -ift, -imp, -ing*, -ink*, -int, -ish, -isk, -ist; -ock*, -omp, -ond; -uck*, -umb, -ump*, -ung, -unk*, -unt, -ush, -ust.	Some words have consonant clusters at the end. Sometimes the sounds of the two consonant letters are blended together [e.g., mask, lump]; other times the two consonant letters stand for one sound (digraph) [e.g., path, sing].										•	•	•	•	•	•									
9 Recognize and use phonograms with vowel combinations (VVC): e.g., -aid, -ail*, -ain*, -ait; -ead, -eak, -eal, -eam, -ean, -eap, -ear, -eat*; -ied, -ief, -ies; -oak, -oat, -oil, -our, -out.	Some words have two vowels together (vowel combination). Sometimes a vowel combination sounds like the name of the first vowel [e.g., stream, road]. Sometimes a vowel combination stands for other sounds [e.g., soil, hour].										•	•	•	•	•	•	•	•							
10 Recognize and use more difficult phonogram patterns in single-syllable words: • VVCC (e.g., paint, fault, reach, beast, speech, tooth, moist, pouch, would, sound, south) • VVCe (e.g., praise, weave, sneeze, noise, loose, mouse) • VCCe (e.g., dance, paste, wedge, judge) • VCCC (e.g., ranch, patch, bench, ditch, lunch) • VVCCe (e.g., pounce) • VVCCC (e.g., caught, launch, health, weight, sought)	Some words have patterns that are the same. Use the spelling pattern to read a word. Use the spelling pattern to write a word.																•	•	•	•	•	•	•		

SPELLING PATTERNS *(continued)*

BEHAVIOR	INSTRUCTIONAL LANGUAGE	PreK			K			1			2			3			4			5			6–8		
		E	M	L	E	M	L	E	M	L	E	M	L	E	M	L	E	M	L	E	M	L	6	7	8
Vowel Phonogram Patterns in Single-Syllable Words																									
11 Recognize and use phonogram patterns with a short vowel sound in single-syllable words: e.g., *-ab, -ack, -ad, -ag, -am, -amp, -an, -and, -ang, -ank, -ant, -ap, -at; -ed, -ell, -en, -end, -ent, -ess, -est, -et; -ick, -id, -ig, -ill, -in, -ing, -ink, -ip, -it; -ob, -ock, -og, -op, -ot; -ub, -uck, -ug, -ump, -un, -unk, -up, -ust, -ut.*	Some words have a short vowel pattern. You can hear the short vowel sound [e.g., cap, best, pick, not, rust].								•	•	•	•	•	•	•	•									
12 Recognize and use phonogram patterns with a long vowel sound in single-syllable words: e.g., *-ace, -ade, -age, -aid, -ail, -ain, -air, -ake, -ale, -ame, -ane, -ape, -ase, -ate, -ave, -ain, -ay, -aze; -e, -ea, -each, -ead, -eak, -eal, -eam, -ean, -eap, -ear, -eat, -ee, -eed, -eek, -eel, -een, -eep, -eer, -eet, -eeze; -ibe, -ice, -ide, -ie, -ied, -ies, -ife, -ight, -ike, -ile, -ime, -ind, -ine, -ipe, -ire, -ise, -ite, -ive, -y, -ye; -o, -oad, -oak, -oal, -oam, -oan, -oar, -oast, -oat, -obe, -ode, -oe, -oke, -old, -ole, -oll, -ome, -one, -ope, -ose, -ost, -ote, -ove, -ow; -ue, -ule, -ume, -use, -ute.*	Some words have a long vowel pattern. You can hear the long vowel sound [e.g., make, green, pie, coat, cute].										•	•	•	•	•	•									
13 Recognize and use phonogram patterns with the /ü/ vowel sound (as in *moon*) in single-syllable words: *-ew, -o, -oo, -ood, -oof, -ool, -oom, -oon, -oop, -oot, -oup.*	Some words have the /ü/ vowel sound as in moon. Several patterns of letters can stand for the /ü/ sound [e.g., flew, do, zoo, soup].													•	•	•	•	•							
14 Recognize and use phonogram patterns with the /u̇/ vowel sound (as in *book*) in single-syllable words: *-ood, -ook, -oot, -ull, -ush.*	Some words have the /u̇/ vowel sound as in book. Several patterns of letters can stand for the /u̇/ vowel sound [e.g., good, pull].													•	•	•	•	•							
15 Recognize and use phonogram patterns with the /ȯ/ vowel sound (as in *saw*) in single-syllable words: e.g., *-alk, -all, -alt, -aw, -awl, -awn, -ong, -oss, -ost, -oth.*	Some words have the /ȯ/ vowel sound as in saw. Several patterns of letters can stand for the /ȯ/ vowel sound [e.g., wall, paw, cost].													•	•	•	•	•	•	•	•				
16 Recognize and use phonogram patterns with vowels and *r* in single-syllable words: e.g., *-air, -ar, -ard, -are, -ark, -arm, -arn, -arp, -art, -ear, -eer, -ir, -ird, -irt, -oor, -ord, -ore, -orn, -ort, -our, -ur, -urn.*	Some words have a vowel pattern with one or two vowels and r. When vowels are with r in words, usually you blend the sound of the vowels with r [e.g., third].													•	•	•	•	•	•	•	•				

BEHAVIOR	INSTRUCTIONAL LANGUAGE	GRADE LEVEL PreK			K			1			2			3			4			5			6–8		
		E	M	L	E	M	L	E	M	L	E	M	L	E	M	L	E	M	L	E	M	L	6	7	8

Vowel Phonogram Patterns in Single-Syllable Words *(continued)*

	BEHAVIOR	INSTRUCTIONAL LANGUAGE	PreK-E	PreK-M	PreK-L	K-E	K-M	K-L	1-E	1-M	1-L	2-E	2-M	2-L	3-E	3-M	3-L	4-E	4-M	4-L	5-E	5-M	5-L	6	7	8
17	Recognize and use phonogram patterns with the /ou/ vowel sound (as in *cow*) in single-syllable words: e.g., *-oud, -our, -out, -ow, -owl, -own*.	*Some words have the /ou/ vowel sound as in* cow. *Several patterns of letters can stand for the /ou/ vowel sound [e.g., pr**ou**d, cl**ow**n].*											●	●	●	●										
18	Recognize and use phonogram patterns with the /oi/ vowel sound (as in *boy*) in single-syllable words: e.g., *-oil, -oin, -oy*.	*Some words have the /oi/ vowel sound as in* boy. *Several patterns of letters can stand for the /oi/ sound [e.g., c**oi**n, j**oy**].*											●	●	●	●										

Assorted Patterns in Multisyllable Words

	BEHAVIOR	INSTRUCTIONAL LANGUAGE	PreK-E	PreK-M	PreK-L	K-E	K-M	K-L	1-E	1-M	1-L	2-E	2-M	2-L	3-E	3-M	3-L	4-E	4-M	4-L	5-E	5-M	5-L	6	7	8
19	Understand and talk about the fact that some words have a double consonant: e.g., *pebble, hidden, earmuff, jiggle, yellow, fulfill, happy, messy, express, bottle, boycott*.	*Some multisyllable words have a double consonant.* *Sometimes a double consonant stands for a consonant sound in the middle of a multisyllable word.* *Sometimes a double consonant stands for a consonant sound at the end of a multisyllable word.*										●	●	●	●	●	●	●	●	●	●	●				
20	Understand and talk about the fact that some words have a pattern with a double consonant that represents two sounds: e.g., *success, accident*.	*Some multisyllable words have a double consonant in the pattern.* *Sometimes a double consonant stands for two consonant sounds in the middle of a multisyllable word.*												●	●	●	●	●	●	●	●	●				
21	Recognize and use frequently appearing syllable patterns in multisyllable words: e.g., *al**one**, **before**, **enter**, **im**itate, **in**crease, re**peat**, un**happy**; trou**ble**, oth**er**, pur**ple**, alread**y***.	*Some syllable patterns appear often in multisyllable words.* *Look for the familiar pattern to read a multisyllable word.* *Think about the familiar pattern to spell a multisyllable word.*												●	●	●	●	●	●	●	●	●				

Vowel Phonogram Patterns in Multisyllable Words

	BEHAVIOR	INSTRUCTIONAL LANGUAGE	PreK-E	PreK-M	PreK-L	K-E	K-M	K-L	1-E	1-M	1-L	2-E	2-M	2-L	3-E	3-M	3-L	4-E	4-M	4-L	5-E	5-M	5-L	6	7	8
22	Recognize and use short vowel phonograms that appear in multisyllable words: e.g., *-ab, -ack, -act, -ad, -ag, -am, -an, -and, -ang, -ank, -ant, -ap, -at; -ed, -ell, -en, -end, -ent, -ess, -est, -et; -ick, -id, -ig, -ill, -in, -ing, -ip, -it; -ob, -ock, -og, -op, -ot; -ub, -uck, -ug, -un, -unk, -up, -ust, -ut*.	*Some multisyllable words have a short vowel pattern. You can hear the short vowel sound in the pattern [e.g., progr**am**, def**end**, perm**it**, forg**ot**, chipm**unk**].*													●	●	●	●	●	●	●	●	●			

SPELLING PATTERNS *(continued)*																									
BEHAVIOR	**INSTRUCTIONAL LANGUAGE**	GRADE LEVEL																							
		PreK			K			1			2			3			4			5			6-8		
		E	M	L	E	M	L	E	M	L	E	M	L	E	M	L	E	M	L	E	M	L	6	7	8

Vowel Phonogram Patterns in Multisyllable Words *(continued)*

#	Behavior	Instructional Language	PreK-E	PreK-M	PreK-L	K-E	K-M	K-L	1-E	1-M	1-L	2-E	2-M	2-L	3-E	3-M	3-L	4-E	4-M	4-L	5-E	5-M	5-L	6	7	8
23	Recognize and use long vowel phonograms that appear in multisyllable words: e.g., -ace, -ade, -age, -aid, -ail, -ain, -ake, -ale, -ame, -ane, -ape, -ase, -ate, -ave, -ay, -aze; -each, -ead, -eal, -eam, -ear, -eat, -ee, -eed, -eel, -een, -eep, -eer, -eet; -ibe, -ice, -ide, -ie, -ied, -ies, -ife, -ight, -ike, -ile, -ime, -ind, -ine, -ipe, -ire, -ise, -ite, -ive, -y; -o, -oad, -oat, -obe, -ode, -oke, -old, -ole, -oll, -one, -ope, -ose, -ost, -ote, -ow; -ue, -uit, -ule, -ume, -use, -ute.	*Some multisyllable words have a long vowel pattern. You can hear the long vowel sound in the pattern [e.g., compl<u>ai</u>n, agr<u>ee</u>, del<u>igh</u>t, aw<u>oke</u>, aven<u>ue</u>].* *There are two slightly different long u sounds. One is the vowel sound heard in flute. The other is the vowel sound heard in cute.*														•	•	•	•	•	•	•	•			
24	Recognize and use unique vowel phonograms that appear in multisyllable words: e.g., -oint, -oy, -ound, -own.	*Some multisyllable words have a unique vowel pattern. You can hear the unique vowel sound in the pattern [e.g., disapp<u>oint</u>, enj<u>oy</u>, ast<u>ound</u>, downt<u>own</u>].*															•	•	•	•	•	•	•			
25	Recognize and use other vowel phonograms that appear in multisyllable words: e.g., -alk, -all, -alt, -aught, -ault, -aw, -awn, -ong, -ought; -ood, -ook, -oot; -oo, -ood, -oof, -ool, -oom, -oon, -oose, -ew; -ead.	*Some multisyllable words have other vowel patterns. You can hear the vowel sound in the pattern [e.g., ass<u>au</u>lt, childh<u>oo</u>d, coc<u>oo</u>n, foreh<u>ea</u>d].*															•	•	•	•	•	•	•	•	•

High-Frequency Words

High-Frequency Words

A core of known high-frequency words is a valuable resource as students build processing strategies for reading and writing. Young children notice words that appear frequently in the simple texts they read; eventually, their recognition of these words becomes automatic. In this way, their reading becomes more efficient, enabling them to decode words using phonics as well as the meaning in the text. These words are powerful examples that help them grasp that a word is always written the same way. They can use known high-frequency words to check on the accuracy of their reading and as resources for solving other words (for example, *this* starts like *the*). In general, students learn the simpler words earlier and in the process develop efficient systems for learning words. They continuously add to the core of high-frequency words they know as they move to late primary and early intermediate grades. Working with high-frequency words helps students look more carefully at words and develop more efficient systems for word recognition. Beyond the intermediate grades, students continue to add known words to their reading and writing vocabularies, but the focus is on commonly misspelled words.

HIGH-FREQUENCY WORDS

BEHAVIOR	INSTRUCTIONAL LANGUAGE	PreK E	PreK M	PreK L	K E	K M	K L	1 E	1 M	1 L	2 E	2 M	2 L	3 E	3 M	3 L	4 E	4 M	4 L	5 E	5 M	5 L	6	7	8
1 Recognize and use high-frequency words with one, two, or three letters: e.g., *a, I, in, is, of, to, and, the.*	Some words have one letter. Some words have two letters. Some words have three letters. You see some words many times when you read. You need to learn words that you see many times because they help you read and write.				•	•	•	•	•	•															
2 Read and write approximately twenty-five high-frequency words.	Read and write high-frequency words.						•	•	•																
3 Locate and read high-frequency words in continuous text.	Find a word when you know how it looks. When you know a word, you can read it every time you see it.						•	•	•	•	•	•	•	•	•	•	•								
4 Recognize and use high-frequency words with three or more letters: e.g., *you, was, for, are, that, with, they, this.*	Some words have three or more letters. You see some words many times when you read. You need to learn words that you see many times because they help you read and write.							•	•	•	•	•	•	•	•										
5 Read and write approximately one hundred high-frequency words.	Read and write high-frequency words.										•	•	•	•											
6 Recognize and use longer high-frequency words, some with more than one syllable: e.g., *after, around, before, their, there, these, very, which.*	Some words have more than one syllable. You need to learn words that you see many times because they help you read and write.													•	•	•	•	•	•	•					

	BEHAVIOR	INSTRUCTIONAL LANGUAGE	GRADE LEVEL																							
			PreK			K			1			2			3			4			5			6–8		
			E	M	L	E	M	L	E	M	L	E	M	L	E	M	L	E	M	L	E	M	L	6	7	8
7	Read and write approximately 200 high-frequency words.	Read and write high-frequency words.											●	●	●	●	●										
8	Develop and use strategies for acquiring a large core of high-frequency words.	Add to the number of high-frequency words you can read and write. Read and write high-frequency words quickly. Check to see how many high-frequency words you know.									●	●	●	●	●	●	●	●	●	●	●						
9	Read and write approximately 500 high-frequency words.	Read and write high-frequency words.													●	●	●	●	●	●	●	●				
10	Recognize commonly misspelled words and rewrite them correctly.	Notice misspelled words and rewrite them correctly.													●	●	●	●	●	●	●	●	●	●	●	●	●

Word Meaning/Vocabulary

Word Meaning/Vocabulary

Students need to know the meanings of the words they are learning to read and write. And they need to have multiple encounters with those words to expand their vocabularies. It is also important for students to develop a more complex understanding of the words they already know. Of course, the meaning of a word often varies with the specific context and can be related to its spelling. Conversely, spelling and pronouncing a word accurately often require students to know the meaning—or meanings—of the word.

In this category of learning, we include concept words and several types of related words, such as synonyms, antonyms, and homonyms (which may be homographs or homophones). Knowing synonyms and antonyms will help students build more powerful systems for connecting and categorizing words; it will also help them comprehend texts better and write in a more interesting way. You will also find principles about word parts. It is essential that students learn to identify the base words in multisyllable words and to understand the meanings of those base words. Also, students need to learn that adding one or more affixes (prefixes and suffixes) to a base word changes the meaning or the function. Separating words into bases and affixes is fundamental to sophisticated word solving. Another powerful source of information for expanding vocabulary is understanding word origins and Greek and Latin word roots and affixes. The historical meanings of these word roots, prefixes, and suffixes are a key to the current meanings and also to understanding cognates (words that are similar in several languages).

WORD MEANING/VOCABULARY

	BEHAVIOR	INSTRUCTIONAL LANGUAGE	GRADE LEVEL																							
			PreK			K			1			2			3			4			5			6-8		
			E	M	L	E	M	L	E	M	L	E	M	L	E	M	L	E	M	L	E	M	L	6	7	8
	Concept Words																									
1	Recognize and use concept words: e.g., color names, number words, days of the week, months of the year, seasons.	*A color (number, day, month, season) has a name.* *Every week the days happen in the same order.* *Every year the months happen in the same order.* *Every year the seasons happen in the same order.* *Read and write the names of colors (numbers, days, months, seasons).* *Find the names of colors (numbers, days, months, seasons).*					•	•	•	•	•															
2	Recognize and use concept words that can have sets and subsets: e.g., *food*: *fruit (apple, pear)*, *vegetable (carrot, pea)*.	*Some words stand for big ideas or items.* *Find words that stand for smaller ideas or items related to the big ideas.*										•	•	•	•	•	•	•	•	•						

WORD MEANING/VOCABULARY *(continued)*

BEHAVIOR	INSTRUCTIONAL LANGUAGE	PreK			K			1			2			3			4			5			6–8		
		E	M	L	E	M	L	E	M	L	E	M	L	E	M	L	E	M	L	E	M	L	6	7	8
Related Words																									
3 Recognize and talk about the fact that words can be related in many ways: • sound: e.g., *hear/here, weather/whether* • spelling: e.g., *bite/kite, increase/release* • category: e.g., *hat/coat, mother/father*	Some words go together because they sound the same. Some words go together because they are spelled the same. Some words go together because they are the same in some way [e.g., clothes, family members].							•	•	•	•	•	•	•	•	•	•	•	•	•	•				
4 Recognize and use synonyms (words that have almost the same meaning): e.g., *mistake/error, destroy/demolish, high/tall, desperately/frantically.*	Some words mean the same. They are synonyms.										•	•	•	•	•	•	•	•	•	•	•	•	•	•	•
5 Recognize and use antonyms (words that have opposite meanings): e.g., *cold/hot, appear/vanish, abundant/scarce, fantasy/reality.*	Some words have opposite meanings. They are antonyms.										•	•	•	•	•	•	•	•	•	•	•				
6 Recognize and use homophones (words that have the same sound, different spellings, and different meanings): e.g., *blew/blue, choral/coral, higher/hire, patience/patients.*	Some words sound the same but have different spellings and meanings. They are homophones.													•	•	•	•	•	•	•	•	•	•	•	•
7 Recognize and use homographs (words that have the same spelling, different meanings and origins, and may have different pronunciations): e.g., *content, duck, flounder, invalid, present, pupil, sewer, temple.*	Some words are spelled the same but have different meanings and origins. Sometimes they are pronounced differently. They are homographs.													•	•	•	•	•	•	•	•	•	•	•	•
8 Recognize and use words with multiple meanings: e.g., *cover, credit, degree, monitor, novel, organ.*	Some words are spelled the same but have more than one meaning.													•	•	•	•	•	•	•	•	•	•	•	•
9 Understand the concept of analogies to determine relationships among words: e.g., • synonyms–*alert : aware :: elevate : raise* • antonyms–*feeble : strong :: durable : flimsy* • homophones–*hoard : horde :: cereal : serial* *(continues)*	Some words are related to other words in specific ways. An analogy shows the relationship between two pairs of words. Think about how a pair of words is related, and think of another pair of words that is related in the same way.																			•	•	•	•	•	•

WORD MEANING/VOCABULARY (continued)

BEHAVIOR	INSTRUCTIONAL LANGUAGE	PreK			K			1			2			3			4			5			6-8		
		E	M	L	E	M	L	E	M	L	E	M	L	E	M	L	E	M	L	E	M	L	6	7	8

Related Words (continued)

	BEHAVIOR	INSTRUCTIONAL LANGUAGE	PreK E	M	L	K E	M	L	1 E	M	L	2 E	M	L	3 E	M	L	4 E	M	L	5 E	M	L	6	7	8
9	(continued) • object/use–*catalog : advertise : : goggles : protect* • part/whole–*chapter : book : : musician : orchestra* • cause/effect–*comedy : laughter : : drought : famine* • member/category–*celery : vegetable : : plumber : occupation* • denotation/connotation– *inexpensive : cheap : : thin : scrawny*	Some words are related to other words in specific ways. An analogy shows the relationship between two pairs of words. Think about how a pair of words is related, and think of another pair of words that is related in the same way.																			●	●	●	●	●	●

Combined and Created Words

	BEHAVIOR	INSTRUCTIONAL LANGUAGE	PreK E	M	L	K E	M	L	1 E	M	L	2 E	M	L	3 E	M	L	4 E	M	L	5 E	M	L	6	7	8
10	Recognize and use compound words: e.g., *blueberry, overhead, snowstorm.*	Some words are made of two smaller words. They are compound words. Each smaller word helps in thinking about the meaning of the whole word.								●	●	●	●	●	●	●	●									
11	Recognize and use compound words with common parts: e.g., *doghouse, housekeeper, schoolhouse; beside, inside, sidewalk; waterfall, watermelon, waterproof.*	Some smaller words appear in many compound words.										●	●	●	●	●	●									
12	Recognize and use portmanteau words, which come from blending two distinct words: e.g., *motel (motor hotel), smash (smack mash), smog (smoke fog).*	Some words are made by blending two other words. The forms and meanings of the two words are blended.																●	●	●	●	●	●	●	●	●
13	Recognize and use clipped words, which come from shortening words: e.g., *ad (advertisement), dorm (dormitory), lab (laboratory), phone (telephone), photo (photograph).*	Some words are made by shortening a longer word.																●	●	●	●	●	●	●	●	●
14	Recognize and use acronyms, which come from combining the initial letter or letters of multiword names or phrases: e.g., *NATO (North Atlantic Treaty Organization), radar (radio detecting and ranging), scuba (self-contained underwater breathing apparatus), UNICEF (United Nations International Children's Emergency Fund).*	Some words are made by combining the first letter or letters of a group of words. They are acronyms.																●	●	●	●	●	●	●	●	●
15	Recognize and discuss the fact that palindromes are words that are spelled the same in either direction: e.g., *gag, kayak, noon.*	Some words are spelled the same forward or backward. They are palindromes.																			●	●	●	●	●	●

WORD MEANING/VOCABULARY (continued)

BEHAVIOR	INSTRUCTIONAL LANGUAGE	PreK			K			1			2			3			4			5			6-8		
		E	M	L	E	M	L	E	M	L	E	M	L	E	M	L	E	M	L	E	M	L	6	7	8
Figurative Uses of Words																									
16 Recognize and use onomatopoetic words: e.g., *buzz, hiss, plop, quack, thump, whack, zoom.*	Some words imitate the sound of a thing or an action. They are onomatopoetic words.													•	•	•	•	•	•	•	•	•			
17 Recognize and discuss the fact that some words have literal and figurative meanings: e.g., • *cold*–"less warm than usual"; "unfriendly" • *shark*–"a large, usually ferocious fish that lives in warm seas"; "a dishonest person who preys on others" • *fork*–"a tool with a handle and two or more long, pointed parts at one end"; "anything shaped like a fork, or any branching"	Some words have a literal meaning and a figurative meaning.															•	•	•	•	•	•	•	•	•	•
18 Recognize and use similes to make a comparison: e.g., • *The child's lovely eyes shone like a pair of moons in the evening sky.* • *The police officer's mood seemed as light as an autumn breeze.*	A simile is a figure of speech that usually uses the word *like* or *as* to compare two unlike things. Similes can make writing more descriptive and interesting.																•	•	•	•	•	•	•	•	•
19 Recognize and use metaphors to make a comparison: e.g., • *My heart became a block of ice.* • *He glimpsed the silver lace of frost on the window.* • *She is a sparkling star.*	A metaphor is a figure of speech that compares two unlike things without the word *like* or *as.* Metaphors can make writing more descriptive and interesting.																•	•	•	•	•	•	•	•	•
20 Recognize and discuss the fact that commonly used idioms that have meanings different from the meanings of the separate words: e.g., *go fly a kite, hold your tongue, on the fence, hit the nail on the head, hit the road, sweat bullets.*	Some expressions have developed meanings that are different from the literal meanings of the words in the expression.																•	•	•	•	•	•	•	•	•
21 Recognize, say, and talk about words that are jumbled for humorous effect: e.g., • spoonerisms–*a lack of pies* for a *pack of lies* • malapropisms–*the very pineapple of politeness* for the *very pinnacle of politeness*	Switching the first letters of words in a phrase can create a humorous effect. This is a spoonerism. Replacing a word with another word that sounds similar but has a different meaning can create a humorous effect. This is a malaprop.																						•	•	•

WORD MEANING/VOCABULARY (continued)

	BEHAVIOR	INSTRUCTIONAL LANGUAGE	GRADE LEVEL																						
			PreK			K			1			2			3			4			5			6-8		
			E	M	L	E	M	L	E	M	L	E	M	L	E	M	L	E	M	L	E	M	L	6	7	8
Parts of Words																										
22	Understand and discuss the concept of suffixes and recognize their use in determining the meaning of some English words: e.g., -able, -al, -ance, -ant, -ar, -arium, -ed, -ence, -ent, -er, -es, -est, -ful, -ial, -ian, -ible, -ic, -ical, -ing, -ion, -ious, -ish, -ist, -ity, -less, -ly, -ment, -ness, -or, -orium, -ous, -s, -sion, -tion, -y.	A suffix is a word part that can be found at the end of many English words. A suffix may contain hints about the meaning of an English word.													●	●	●	●	●	●	●	●	●	●	●	●
23	Understand and discuss the concept of prefixes and recognize their use in determining the meaning of some English words: e.g., ad-, ant-, ante-, anti-, bi-, circu-, com-, con-, contra-, contro-, counter-, dec-, dis-, em-, en-, ex-, fore-, in-, inter-, intra-, mal-, mis-, mon-, mono-, multi-, non-, oct-, pent-, per-, poly-, post-, pre-, quadr-, re-, sub-, super-, trans-, tri-, un-, uni-.	A prefix is a word part that can be found at the beginning of many English words. A prefix may contain hints about the meaning of an English word.														●	●	●	●	●	●	●	●	●	●	●
Word Origins																										
24	Develop interest in vocabulary by recognizing and appreciating aspects of words and by "collecting" and discussing interesting words and using them in conversation.	Discovering new words can be fun and exciting. Thinking about where words come from can be fascinating.														●	●	●	●	●	●	●	●	●	●	●
25	Understand and discuss the fact that cognates are words in different languages that have similar meanings and spellings because they have related origins: e.g., English alphabet, French alphabet, Italian alfabeto, German Alphabet.	Some words appear in different languages with very similar spellings and meanings. They are cognates. Cognates have related word origins.															●	●	●	●	●	●	●	●	●	●
26	Understand and discuss the fact that English words or terms are derived from many different sources, such as other languages, technology, names, trademarked products, and social practices: e.g., tortilla, parliament, harmonica, khaki, algebra; blog, hashtag, hyperlink; sandwich, valentine, hamburger; xerox, jeep, Band-Aid, Kleenex; fist bump, social media, takeout.	Over many years, English words or terms have been added from other languages, new technologies, the names of people and places, trademarked products, and social practices.																●	●	●	●	●	●	●	●	●

WORD MEANING/VOCABULARY *(continued)*

BEHAVIOR	INSTRUCTIONAL LANGUAGE	GRADE LEVEL																							
		PreK			K			1			2			3			4			5			6-8		
		E	M	L	E	M	L	E	M	L	E	M	L	E	M	L	E	M	L	E	M	L	6	7	8

Word Origins *(continued)*

	BEHAVIOR	INSTRUCTIONAL LANGUAGE	PreK E	PreK M	PreK L	K E	K M	K L	1 E	1 M	1 L	2 E	2 M	2 L	3 E	3 M	3 L	4 E	4 M	4 L	5 E	5 M	5 L	6	7	8
27	Understand and discuss the concept of Latin roots and recognize their use in determining the meanings of some English words: e.g., *aqua, aud, bene, cap, centr, clos, clud, clus, corp, cred, dict, duc, duct, dur, equa, equi, fac, fer, fic, fin, firm, flect, flex, form, fract, frag, grad, gress, hab, hib, ject, join, junct, loc, luc, lum, man, mem, min, miss, mit, mob, mot, mov, ped, pel, pend, pens, pon, pop, port, pos, prim, prin, pub, puls, quer, ques, quir, quis, rupt, scribe, script, sens, sent, sign, sist, sol, son, spec, sta, stat, stit, stru, struct, tain, tempo, ten, tent, tin, terr, tract, val, ven, vent, ver, vers, vert, vid, vis, voc, vok.*	*A root is a word part from another language. Roots can be found in most English words.* *A word root may contain hints about the meaning of an English word.* *Many English words come from Latin. They have Latin roots.*																		•	•	•	•	•	•	•
28	Understand and discuss the concept of Greek roots and recognize their use in determining the meaning of some English words: e.g., *aer, arch, aster, astr, astro, bio, chron, cycl, dem, geo, gram, graph, hydr, hydro, log, mega, meter, micro, ology, phon, photo, pod, pol, poli, polis, scop, scope, tele, therm.*	*A root is a word part from another language. Roots can be found in most English words.* *A word root may contain hints about the meaning of an English word.* *Many English words come from Greek. They have Greek roots.*																			•	•	•	•	•	•
29	Recognize and use prefixes, suffixes, and word roots that have Greek and Latin origins to understand word meaning: e.g., *incredible–in-* ("not"), Latin *cred* ("believe"), and *-ible* ("capable of"); *antibiotic–anti-* ("opposite" or "against"), Greek *bio* ("life"), and *-ic* ("related to").	*Some Latin or Greek roots can be combined with affixes to create other words.* *Recognizing prefixes, suffixes, and Latin or Greek roots is helpful to understand the meanings of words.*																			•	•	•	•	•	•
30	Recognize and discuss the fact that words in different languages or in the same language may have a common origin: e.g., *escribir* (Spanish "to write"), *describe*, and *script* derive from Latin *scribere*, "to write."	*Some English words have the same origin as words from other languages.* *Some English words are related to each other because they have the same origin.*																			•	•	•	•	•	

Word Structure

Word Structure

Looking at the structure of words will help students learn how words are related to each other and how they can be changed by adding letters, letter clusters, and larger word parts. Being able to recognize syllables, for example, helps readers and writers break down words into smaller units that are easier to analyze.

Words often have *affixes*, parts added before or after a word to change its meaning or function. An affix can be a prefix or a suffix. The word to which affixes are added can be a word root or a base word. A *base word* is a complete word; a *word root* is a word part that may have Greek or Latin origins (such as *phon* in *telephone*). It will not be necessary for young children to make this distinction when they are beginning to learn about simple affixes, but working with suffixes and prefixes will help children read and understand words that include affixes as well as use them accurately in writing.

Endings or word parts that are added to base words signal meaning and function. For example, they may signal relationships (*prettier/prettiest*), time (*planting/planted*), or grammatical function (*equal/equalize*). Principles related to word structure include understanding the meaning and structure of compound words, contractions, plurals, and possessives as well as knowing how to form and use them accurately. We have also included common abbreviations that students often see in the books they read and want to use in their writing.

	BEHAVIOR	INSTRUCTIONAL LANGUAGE	PreK E	PreK M	PreK L	K E	K M	K L	1 E	1 M	1 L	2 E	2 M	2 L	3 E	3 M	3 L	4 E	4 M	4 L	5 E	5 M	5 L	6-8 6	6-8 7	6-8 8
	Syllables																									
1	Understand and talk about the concept of a syllable.	A syllable is a word part you can hear.					•	•	•	•	•	•														
2	Hear, say, clap, and identify syllables in one- or two-syllable words: e.g., *big, frog, gold; lit/tle, mon/key, sil/ver.*	Listen for the syllables in words. Some words have one syllable. Some words have more than one syllable. Look at the syllables in a word to read it. Say and clap the syllables to notice them in a word.						•	•	•	•	•	•	•												
3	Understand and talk about the fact that each syllable contains one vowel sound.	Each syllable in a word has a vowel sound.										•	•	•												
4	Recognize and use syllables in words with double consonants: e.g., *ap/ple, bot/tle, tun/nel.*	When a word has double consonants in the middle, divide the syllables between the consonants.											•	•	•	•	•	•								
5	Hear, say, clap, and identify syllables in words with three or more syllables: e.g., *an/oth/er, bi/cy/cle, fish/er/man, par/a/graph; el/e/va/tor, un/u/su/al, wat/er/mel/on.*	Listen for the syllables in words. Look at the syllables in a word to read it. Say and clap the syllables to identify them in a word.											•	•	•	•	•	•	•	•	•	•				

WORD STRUCTURE (continued)

BEHAVIOR	INSTRUCTIONAL LANGUAGE	PreK			K			1			2			3			4			5			6-8		
		E	M	L	E	M	L	E	M	L	E	M	L	E	M	L	E	M	L	E	M	L	6	7	8

Syllables (continued)

	BEHAVIOR	INSTRUCTIONAL LANGUAGE	PreK E	PreK M	PreK L	K E	K M	K L	1 E	1 M	1 L	2 E	2 M	2 L	3 E	3 M	3 L	4 E	4 M	4 L	5 E	5 M	5 L	6	7	8
6	Recognize and use open syllables–syllables that end with a single vowel, which usually represents a long vowel sound: e.g., o/pen, pi/lot, ti/ger.	When a syllable ends with a single vowel, the vowel sound is usually long.													•	•	•	•	•	•	•					
7	Recognize and use closed syllables–syllables that end with a consonant and usually have a short vowel sound: e.g., can/dle, fif/teen, mod/ern.	When a syllable ends with a vowel and a consonant, the vowel sound is usually short.													•	•	•	•	•	•	•					
8	Recognize and use r-influenced syllables–syllables that contain one or two vowels followed by the letter r: e.g., a/part/ment, dirt/y, for/get, four/teen, gar/bage, prair/ie.	Some words have one or two vowels followed by the letter r. The letter r changes the vowel sound. The vowel(s) and the letter r stay together in the same syllable.													•	•	•	•	•	•	•					
9	Recognize and use vowel combination syllables–syllables that contain two or more letters together that represent one vowel sound: e.g., be/tween, en/joy, mid/night.	Some words have two or more letters together that represent one vowel sound. The letters usually stay together in the same syllable.													•	•	•	•	•	•	•					
10	Recognize and use VCe syllables–syllables that contain a (long) vowel followed by a consonant and then silent e: e.g., be/side, eve/ning, in/vite, lone/ly, stam/pede, state/ment.	Some words have a vowel followed by a consonant and then a silent e. The pattern stays together in a syllable, and the vowel sound is long.													•	•	•	•	•	•	•					
11	Recognize and use consonant + le syllables–syllables that contain a consonant followed by the letters le: e.g., a/ble, ea/gle, scram/ble, tem/ple.	When a consonant is followed by the letters le at the end of a word, the consonant plus the letters le usually form the final syllable.													•	•	•	•	•	•	•	•				
12	Recognize and use syllables in words with the VCCV pattern (syllable juncture): e.g., ber/ry, both/er, dis/may, hel/met.	When there are two consonants in the middle of a word, break the word between the consonants, but keep digraphs together.													•	•	•	•	•	•	•	•				
13	Recognize and use syllables in words with the VCCCV pattern (syllable juncture): e.g., emp/ty, hun/dred, king/dom, mon/ster.	When there are three consonants in the middle of a word, break the word between the consonants, but keep digraphs or consonant clusters together.													•	•	•	•	•	•	•	•				
14	Recognize and use syllables in words with the VV pattern: e.g., gi/ant, ru/in, sci/ence.	When a word has two vowels together and you can hear two vowel sounds, break the word between the vowels.														•	•	•	•	•	•	•				

WORD STRUCTURE (continued)

BEHAVIOR	INSTRUCTIONAL LANGUAGE	PreK			K			1			2			3			4			5			6-8		
		E	M	L	E	M	L	E	M	L	E	M	L	E	M	L	E	M	L	E	M	L	6	7	8
Compound Words																									
15 Recognize and use common compound words: e.g., *cannot, into, maybe, myself, sometimes, something, today, without, yourself.*	Some words are made of two smaller words and are called compound words.								•	•	•	•	•	•											
16 Recognize and use other compound words: e.g., *airport, birthday, blueberry, flashlight, highway, homesick, peanut, railroad, sidewalk, snowstorm.*	The word parts in a compound word often give hints about the meaning of the compound word.										•	•	•	•	•	•	•								
17 Recognize and use compound words that have frequently used words: e.g., *anybody, anymore, anyone, anything, anytime, anyway, anywhere; everybody, everyday, everyone, everything, everywhere; somebody, someday, somehow, someone, someplace, something, sometime, somewhat, somewhere.*	Some frequently used words appear often in compound words. Make connections among compound words that have the same word parts.										•	•	•	•	•	•	•	•							
18 Recognize and use compound words that have common parts: e.g., • *bookcase, bookmark, bookshelf, notebook, scrapbook, textbook* • *countdown, download, downstairs, downtown, facedown, sundown* • *campfire, firefighter, firehouse, fireplace, firewood, wildfire*	Some compound words have common parts. The common part can appear at the beginning of the word or at the end of the word. Make connections among compound words that have common word parts.										•	•	•	•	•	•	•	•							
Contractions																									
19 Understand and talk about the concept of a contraction.	A contraction is one or more words put together. A letter or letters are left out, and an apostrophe takes the place of the missing letter or letters.								•	•	•	•	•												
20 Recognize and use contractions with *not*: e.g., *aren't, can't, couldn't, didn't, doesn't, don't, hadn't, hasn't, haven't, isn't, shouldn't, wasn't, weren't, wouldn't.*	Some contractions are made with *not*. To write a contraction with not, leave out the letter o and put an apostrophe in its place.								•	•	•	•	•	•	•	•	•								

		GRADE LEVEL																					
BEHAVIOR	**INSTRUCTIONAL LANGUAGE**	PreK			K			1			2			3			4			5			6–8		
		E	M	L	E	M	L	E	M	L	E	M	L	E	M	L	E	M	L	E	M	L	6	7	8
Contractions *(continued)*																									
21 Recognize and use contractions with *am* and *are*: *I'm; we're, you're, they're.*	Some contractions are made with am. To write a contraction with am, leave out the letter a and put an apostrophe in its place. Some contractions are made with are. To write a contraction with are, leave out the letter a and put an apostrophe in its place.							•	•	•	•	•	•	•	•	•	•								
22 Recognize and use contractions with *is* or *has*: e.g., *he's, she's, it's, how's, that's, there's, what's, where's, who's.*	Some contractions are made with is. To write a contraction with is, leave out the letter i and put an apostrophe in its place. Some contractions are made with has. To write a contraction with has, leave out the letters ha and put an apostrophe in place of those missing letters. Since contractions with is and has look the same, use the context to know which two words were used to make the contraction.							•	•	•	•	•	•	•	•	•	•								
23 Recognize and use contractions with *will*: e.g., *I'll, we'll, you'll, he'll, she'll, it'll, they'll, that'll, who'll.*	Some contractions are made with will. To write a contraction with will, leave out the letters wi and put an apostrophe in their place.							•	•	•	•	•	•	•	•	•	•								
24 Recognize and use contractions with *have*: e.g., *I've, we've, you've, they've, could've, should've, would've.*	Some contractions are made with have. To write a contraction with have, leave out the letters ha and put an apostrophe in their place.										•	•	•	•	•	•	•	•	•	•					
25 Recognize and use contractions with *had* or *would*: e.g., *I'd, we'd, you'd, he'd, she'd, they'd, there'd, who'd.*	Some contractions are made with had. To write a contraction with had, leave out the letters ha and put an apostrophe in their place. Some contractions are made with would. To write a contraction with would, leave out the letters woul and put an apostrophe in their place. Since contractions with would and had look the same, use the context to know which two words were used to make the contraction.																•	•	•	•	•				
26 Recognize and discuss multiple contractions with *not* and *have* (almost solely in oral language): e.g., *mustn't've, shouldn't've, wouldn't've.*	Sometimes in oral language a contraction is made up of three words. Letters are left out of the second and third words, and apostrophes would be used in place of those missing letters. Multiple contractions are usually made with not and have.																			•	•	•	•	•	•

WORD STRUCTURE (continued)

BEHAVIOR	INSTRUCTIONAL LANGUAGE	PreK			K			1			2			3			4			5			6-8		
		E	M	L	E	M	L	E	M	L	E	M	L	E	M	L	E	M	L	E	M	L	6	7	8
Plurals																									
27 Understand and talk about the fact that a noun can refer to more than one person, place, or thing: e.g., *fathers, towns, toys.*	Plural means "more than one."						•	•	•																
28 Recognize and use plurals that add -s: e.g., *books, cars, dogs, farms, mothers, zoos.*	Add -s to some words to make them plural. You can hear the s at the end of the word.						•	•	•																
29 Recognize and use plurals that add -es to words that end with the letters *ch, sh, s, x,* or *z:* e.g., *branches, dishes, classes, boxes, buzzes.*	Add -es to words that end with ch, sh, s, x, and z to make them plural.							•	•	•	•	•	•	•											
30 Recognize and use plurals that add -s to words that end with a vowel and *y:* e.g., *boys, chimneys, holidays.*	Add -s to words that end with a vowel and y to make them plural.										•	•	•	•	•	•									
31 Recognize and use plurals that add -es to words that end with a consonant and *y* after changing the *y* to *i:* e.g., *countries, jellies, rubies.*	When a word ends with a consonant and y, change the y to i and add -es to make the word plural.													•	•	•	•	•	•						
32 Recognize and use plurals that add -es to words after changing the final *f* or *fe* to *v:* e.g., *knives, scarves, wolves.*	For most words ending with f or fe, change the f or fe to v and add -es to make the words plural.													•	•	•	•	•							
33 Recognize and use irregular plurals that change the spelling of the word: e.g., *goose/geese, mouse/mice, ox/oxen, woman/women.*	Change the spelling of some words to make them plural.													•	•	•	•	•	•	•	•	•			
34 Recognize and use irregular plurals that are the same as the singular form of the word: e.g., *deer, moose, salmon, sheep.*	Some words are spelled the same in both the singular form and the plural form.													•	•	•	•	•	•	•	•				
35 Recognize and use plurals that add -s to words that end with *o:* e.g., *pianos, rodeos.*	Add -s to most words that end with o to make them plural. Some words that end with o have two plural forms—e.g., zeros, zeroes.																•	•	•	•	•				
36 Recognize and use plurals that add -es to words that end with a consonant and *o:* e.g., *echoes, heroes.*	Add -es to a few words that end in a consonant and o to make them plural. Some words that end with o have two plural forms—e.g., volcanoes, volcanos.																•	•	•	•	•				

BEHAVIOR	INSTRUCTIONAL LANGUAGE	GRADE LEVEL																						
		PreK			K			1			2			3			4			5			6-8		
		E	M	L	E	M	L	E	M	L	E	M	L	E	M	L	E	M	L	E	M	L	6	7	8

Plurals (continued)

| 37 | Recognize and use irregular plurals that are formed by changing the final letters of the base word: e.g., *crisis, crises; medium, media; cactus, cacti.* | *Change the spelling of some words to make them plural.* *For some words that end with is, change the final is to es.* *For some words that end with um, change the final um to a.* *For some words that end with us, change the final us to i.* | | | | | | | | | | | | | | | | | | | • | • | • | • | • | • |

Possessives

| 38 | Recognize and use possessives that add an apostrophe and s to singular nouns (including proper nouns) to show ownership: e.g., *boy's popcorn, Pat's neck, town's library, whale's eyes.* | *Possess means "have or own." A person, place, or thing can possess something.* *Add an apostrophe and s to a singular noun to show possession.* | | | | | | | | | | • | • | • | • | | | | | | | | | | | |

| 39 | Recognize and use possessives that add an apostrophe and s to singular nouns (including proper nouns) that end with s to show ownership: e.g., *princess's closet, Texas's flag, harness's buckle, its whiskers.* | *Add an apostrophe and s to a name that ends in s to show possession.* *Add an apostrophe and s to a singular noun that ends in s to show possession.* *Do not add an apostrophe and s to the possessive pronoun its.* | | | | | | | | | | | | | | • | • | • | • | • | • | | | | | |

| 40 | Recognize and use possessives that add an apostrophe to plural nouns that end with s to show ownership: e.g., *girls' disappointment, universities' cafeterias, woodpeckers' clatter.* | *Add an apostrophe to a plural noun that ends in s to show possession by more than one person, place, or thing.* | | | | | | | | | | | | | | | | • | • | • | • | • | • | • | | |

| 41 | Recognize and use possessives that add an apostrophe and s to irregular plural nouns to show ownership: e.g., *oxen's strength, women's jackets.* | *Some plural nouns do not end with an s.* *Add an apostrophe and s to a plural noun that does not end in s to show possession by more than one person or thing.* | | | | | | | | | | | | | | | | • | • | • | • | | | | | |

Suffixes

| 42 | Understand and talk about the concept of a suffix. | *A suffix is a letter or a group of letters put at the end of a word root or base word to change its meaning or its function.* *Sometimes a suffix changes a base word into an adjective, an adverb, a noun, or a verb.* *Sometimes a suffix changes a verb to show when something happens.* | | | | | | | | | | • | • | • | • | • | • | • | • | • | • | • | • | • | • | • |

		GRADE LEVEL																						
BEHAVIOR	**INSTRUCTIONAL LANGUAGE**	PreK			K			1			2			3			4			5			6–8		
		E	M	L	E	M	L	E	M	L	E	M	L	E	M	L	E	M	L	E	M	L	6	7	8

Suffixes *(continued)*

43 Understand and talk about the fact that several basic rules govern the spelling of words with suffixes:

- For many words, there are no spelling changes when adding a suffix: e.g., *run/runs, bright/brighter/brightest, moist/moisten, final/finally, teach/teacher*
- For words that end with silent *e*, usually drop the *e* when adding a suffix that begins with a vowel, but usually keep the *e* when adding a suffix that begins with a consonant: e.g., *live/living* but *live/lives, fierce/fiercer/fiercest, sterile/sterilize, please/pleasant* but *grace/graceful, bake/baker* but *aware/awareness*
- For one-syllable words that end with a single vowel and one consonant, usually double the final consonant when adding a suffix that begins with a vowel, but usually do not double the final consonant when adding a suffix that begins with a consonant: e.g., *sad/sadder/saddest* and *flat/flatten* and *pet/petted* and *beg/begger* but *sin/sinful* and *fit/fitness.*
- For multisyllable words with an accented final syllable that ends with a single vowel and one consonant, follow the rules for one-syllable words: *remit/remitting* but *remit/remits, excel/excellent* but *excel/excels, admit/admittance* but *admit/admits, commit/commitment* but *commit/commits*

(continues)

Instructional Language: Use the basic rules to spell words correctly when adding suffixes.

Dots marked across Grade 2 (E) through Grade 6–8 (8).

WORD STRUCTURE

		GRADE LEVEL																								
BEHAVIOR	**INSTRUCTIONAL LANGUAGE**	PreK			K			1			2			3			4			5			6–8		
		E	M	L	E	M	L	E	M	L	E	M	L	E	M	L	E	M	L	E	M	L	6	7	8

WORD STRUCTURE (continued)

Suffixes (continued)

43 (continued)
- For multisyllable words with an unaccented final syllable that ends with a single vowel and one consonant, usually do not double the final consonant when adding a suffix: e.g., *visit/visited, slender/slenderer, civil/civilize, vigil/vigilant, limit/limitless, develop/developer*
- For words that end with a consonant and *y*, usually change the *y* to *i* and add the suffix, but for words that end with a vowel and *y*, usually keep the *y* and add the suffix: e.g., *copy/copied* but *enjoy/enjoyed; crazy/crazier/craziest* but *coy/coyer/coyest; identify/identifiable* but *pay/payable, carry/carrier* but *employ/employer*

Use the basic rules to spell words correctly when adding suffixes.

Marks (row 43): 2E • 2M • 2L • 3E • 3M • 3L • 4E • 4M • 4L • 5E • 5M • 5L • 6 • 7 • 8 •

Suffixes: Inflectional Endings

44 Recognize and use the ending *-s* when making a verb agree with its subject: e.g., *cats run/cat runs, they jump/she jumps, dogs play/dog plays.*

Sometimes -s is added to the end of a verb to make it sound right in a sentence.

Marks (row 44): 2E • 2M •

45 Recognize and use the ending *-es* when making a verb agree with its subject: e.g., *they miss/she misses; children splash/child splashes; boys search/boy searches, they cry/he cries.*

Sometimes -es is added to the end of a verb to make it sound right in a sentence.

Marks (row 45): 2L • 3E • 3M • 4E • 4M •

		WORD STRUCTURE *(continued)*																								
			GRADE LEVEL																							
	BEHAVIOR	**INSTRUCTIONAL LANGUAGE**	PreK		K			1			2			3			4			5			6-8			
			E	M	L	E	M	L	E	M	L	E	M	L	E	M	L	E	M	L	E	M	L	6	7	8
Suffixes: Inflectional Endings *(continued)*																										
46	Recognize and use the ending *-ing* when forming the present participle of a verb: e.g., help/helping, live/living, grin/grinning, remit/remitting, visit/visiting, copy/copying, enjoy/enjoying, mix/mixing, panic/panicking.	*Add -ing to the end of some verbs to show that something is happening now.* *Use the basic rules to spell words correctly when adding the suffix -ing.* *When adding the suffix -ing to a word that ends in y, keep the y and add -ing no matter if the y is preceded by a vowel or a consonant.* *Sometimes the suffix -ing requires the use of additional spelling rules:* • *For verbs that end with a single vowel and the consonant x, you do not double the x before adding -ing.* • *For verbs ending with hard c, add a k before adding the ending -ing.*						•	•	•	•	•	•	•	•	•	•	•	•									
47	Recognize and use the ending *-ed* when forming the past tense of a verb: e.g., help/helped, live/lived, grin/grinned, remit/remitted, visit/visited, copy/copied, enjoy/enjoyed, mix/mixed, panic/panicked.	*Add -ed to the end of some verbs to show that something already happened.* *Think about how to spell words correctly when you add the suffix -ed.* *Sometimes the suffix -ed requires the use of additional spelling rules:* • *For verbs that end with a single vowel and the consonant x, you do not double the the x before adding -ed.* • *For verbs ending with hard c, add a k before adding the ending -ed.*						•	•	•	•	•	•	•	•	•	•	•	•									
48	Understand and talk about the fact that the ending *-ed* when forming the past tense of a verb can represent several different sounds: e.g., *closed, added, walked.*	*When -ed is added to a verb, sometimes it sounds like /d/.* *When -ed is added to a verb, sometimes it sounds like /ed/.* *When -ed is added to a verb, sometimes it sounds like /t/.*									•	•	•	•	•	•	•										
49	Recognize and use the ending *-ing* with multisyllable verbs with an accented last syllable when forming the present participle of a verb: e.g., *remind/reminding, decline/declining, remit/remitting, rely/relying, enjoy/enjoying.*	*Add -ing to the end of some multisyllable verbs with an accented last syllable to show that something is happening now.* *Use the basic rules to spell words correctly when adding the suffix -ing.* *When adding the suffix -ing to a verb that ends in y, keep the y and add -ing no matter if the y is preceded by a vowel or a consonant.*															•	•	•	•	•	•	•	•	•	•
50	Recognize and use the ending *-ed* with multisyllable verbs with an accented last syllable when forming the past tense of a verb: e.g., *remind/reminded, decline/declined, remit/remitted, rely/relied, enjoy/enjoyed.*	*Add -ed to the end of some multisyllable verbs with an accented last syllable to show that something already happened.* *Use the basic rules to spell words correctly when adding the suffix -ed.*															•	•	•	•	•	•	•	•	•	•

WORD STRUCTURE

BEHAVIOR	INSTRUCTIONAL LANGUAGE	PreK E	PreK M	PreK L	K E	K M	K L	1 E	1 M	1 L	2 E	2 M	2 L	3 E	3 M	3 L	4 E	4 M	4 L	5 E	5 M	5 L	6	7	8
Suffixes: Inflectional Endings (continued)																									
51 Recognize and use the ending -ing with multisyllable verbs with an accent not on the last syllable when forming the present participle of a verb: e.g., cherish/cherishing, locate/locating, differ/differing, rely/relying, enjoy/enjoying, panic/panicking.	Add -ing to the end of some multisyllable verbs in which the accent is not on the last syllable to show that something is happening now. Use the basic rules to spell words correctly when adding the suffix -ing. When adding the suffix -ing to a verb that ends in y, keep the y and add -ing no matter if the y is preceded by a vowel or a consonant. Sometimes the suffix -ing requires the use of additional spelling rules: • For verbs ending with hard c, add a k before adding the ending -ing.																•	•	•	•	•	•	•	•	•
52 Recognize and use the ending -ed with multisyllable verbs with an accent not on the last syllable when forming the past tense of a verb: e.g., cherish/cherished, locate/located, differ/differed, rely/relied, enjoy/enjoyed, panic/panicked.	Add -ed to the end of some multisyllable verbs in which the accent is not on the last syllable to show that something already happened. Use the basic rules to spell words correctly when adding the suffix -ed. Sometimes the suffix -ed requires the use of additional spelling rules: • For verbs ending with hard c, add a k before adding the ending -ed.																•	•	•	•	•	•	•	•	•
Suffixes: Comparative Endings																									
53 Recognize and use the suffixes -er and -est to show comparison: e.g., bright/brighter/brightest, fierce/fiercer/fiercest, sad/sadder/saddest, slender/slenderer/slenderest, crazy/crazier/craziest, coy/coyer/coyest.	Add the suffix -er to the end of a base word to show comparison between two things. Add the suffix -est to the end of a base word to show comparison among three or more things. Use the basic rules to spell words correctly when adding the suffixes -er and -est.														•	•	•	•	•	•	•				
Suffixes: Verb Suffixes																									
54 Recognize and use the suffix -en, meaning "to make or become" or "to give or gain," to form a verb: e.g., moist/moisten, haste/hasten, flat/flatten.	Add the suffix -en to the end of a base word to mean "to make or become" or "to give or gain." Use the basic rules to spell words correctly when adding the suffix -en.																						•	•	•
55 Recognize and use the suffix -ize, meaning "to make or become," to form a verb: e.g., equal/equalize, sterile/sterilize, civil/civilize, apology/apologize, bapt/baptize.	Add the suffix -ize to the end of a word root or a base word to mean "to make or become." Use the basic rules to spell words correctly when adding the suffix -ize.																						•	•	•

WORD STRUCTURE

			WORD STRUCTURE *(continued)*																				

WORD STRUCTURE

	BEHAVIOR	INSTRUCTIONAL LANGUAGE	PreK			K			1			2			3			4			5			6–8		
			E	M	L	E	M	L	E	M	L	E	M	L	E	M	L	E	M	L	E	M	L	6	7	8

Suffixes: Adjective and Adverb Suffixes

56	Recognize and use the suffix -*ly*, meaning "in a specific manner, period of time, or order," to form an adverb: e.g., *frequent/frequently, live/lively, sad/sadly, livid/lividly, easy/easily, notable/notably, automatic/automatically.*	Add the suffix -ly to some base words to make words that tell how something is done (adverbs). Add the suffix -ly to some base words to mean "in a specific manner, period of time, or order." Use the basic rules to spell words correctly when adding the suffix -ly. An exception to the basic rules is for words that end with a consonant and le, drop the e and add y. Sometimes the suffix -ly requires the use of additional spelling rules: • For words that end in ic, add al before adding -ly.														●	●	●	●	●	●	●	●	●	●	●	●
57	Recognize and use the suffix -*y*, meaning "having or containing," to form an adjective: e.g., *dirt/dirty, ache/achy, knot/knotty, velvet/velvety.*	Add the suffix -y to some base words to form adjectives. Add the suffix -y to some base words to mean "having or containing." Use the basic rules to spell words correctly when adding the suffix -y.															●	●	●	●							
58	Recognize and use the suffix -*ish*, meaning "like," "somewhat," or "relating to," to form an adjective: e.g., *self/selfish, blue/bluish, big/biggish, woman/womanish, baby/babyish, boy/boyish.*	Add the suffix -ish to some base words to form adjectives. Add the suffix -ish to the end of a base word to mean "like," "somewhat," or "relating to." Use the basic rules to spell words correctly when adding the suffix -ish. When adding the suffix -ish to a word that ends in y, keep the y and add -ish no matter if the y is preceded by a vowel or a consonant.															●	●	●								
59	Recognize and use the suffixes -*able* and -*ible*, meaning "capable of," to form an adjective: • Add -*able* to base words: e.g., *afford/affordable, enforce/enforceable, hit/hittable, commit/committable, credit/creditable, identify/identifiable, portray/portrayable.* • Add -*ible* to word roots: e.g., *terr/terrible, vis/visible, sens/sensible, flex/flexible, aud/audible.*	Add the suffix -able or -ible to some word roots or base words to form adjectives. Add the suffix -able to the end of a base word to mean "capable of." Add the suffix -ible to the end of a word root to mean "capable of." Add the suffix -ible to a word root with no spelling changes. Use the basic rules to spell words correctly when adding the suffix -able. Sometimes the suffix -able requires the use of additional spelling rules: • For words that end with ce or ge, keep the e and add the suffix -able.																		●	●	●	●	●	●	●

BEHAVIOR	INSTRUCTIONAL LANGUAGE	GRADE LEVEL																						
		PreK			K			1			2			3			4			5			6–8		
		E	M	L	E	M	L	E	M	L	E	M	L	E	M	L	E	M	L	E	M	L	6	7	8

Suffixes: Adjective and Adverb Suffixes *(continued)*

60 Recognize and use the suffixes *-ful,* meaning "full of," and *-less,* meaning "without," to form an adjective: • -ful: e.g., *fear/fearful, care/careful, sin/sinful, forget/forgetful, pocket/pocketful, pity/pitiful, joy/joyful* • -less: e.g., *fear/fearless, care/careless, brim/brimless, limit/limitless pity/pitiless, joy/joyless*	Add the suffix -ful or -less to some base words to form adjectives. Add the suffix -ful to the end of a base word to mean "full of something." Add the suffix -less to the end of a base word to mean "without." Use the basic rules to spell words correctly when adding the suffixes -ful and -less.																	●	●	●	●	●	●	●
61 Recognize and use the suffixes *-ant* and *-ent,* meaning "characterized by" or "inclined to," to form an adjective: • -ant: e.g., *import/important, ignore/ignorant, vigil/vigilant, rely/reliant, buoy/buoyant* • -ent: e.g., *insist/insistent, urge/urgent, excel/excellent, differ/different*	Add the suffix -ant or -ent to some base words to form adjectives. When used to form an adjective, the suffix -ant or -ent means "characterized by" or "inclined to." Use the basic rules to spell words correctly when adding the suffixes -ant and -ent.																	●	●	●	●	●	●	●
62 Recognize and use the suffixes *-ous* and *-ious,* meaning "full of," "like," or "having the quality of," to form an adjective: • -ous: e.g., *humor/humorous, adventure/adventurous, fury/furious, joy/joyous, courage/courageous* • -ious: e.g., *grace/gracious, prestige/prestigious*	Add the suffix -ous or -ious to some base words to form adjectives. Add the suffix -ous or -ious to the end of a base word to mean "full of," "like," or "having the quality of." Use the basic rules to spell words correctly when adding the suffixes -ous and -ious. Sometimes the suffixes -ous and -ious require the use of additional spelling rules: • For words that end with ce or ge, keep the e and add -ous. • For words that end with ce or ge, drop the e and add the suffix -ious.																	●	●	●	●	●	●	●

WORD STRUCTURE (continued)

Suffixes: Adjective and Adverb Suffixes (continued)

#	BEHAVIOR	INSTRUCTIONAL LANGUAGE	PreK			K			1			2			3			4			5			6–8		
			E	M	L	E	M	L	E	M	L	E	M	L	E	M	L	E	M	L	E	M	L	6	7	8
63	Recognize and use the suffixes -al, -ial, -ian, -ic, and -ical, meaning "like," "related to," or "suitable for," to form an adjective: • -al: e.g., emotion/emotional, globe/global, refer/referral, clinic/clinical, ceremony/ceremonial, loc/local • -ial: e.g., part/partial, finance/financial, editor/editorial, spec/special • -ian: e.g., civil/civilian, reptile/reptilian, grammar/grammarian • -ic: e.g., hero/heroic, athlete/athletic, magnet/magnetic, chron/chronic • -ical: e.g., myth/mythical, type/typical, biography/biographical, log/logical	*Add the suffix -al, -ial, -ian, -ic, or -ical to some nouns or word roots to form adjectives.* *Add the suffix -al, -ial, -ian, -ic, or -ical to the end of a base word or a word root to mean "like," "related to," or "suitable for."* *Use the basic rules to spell words correctly when adding the suffixes -al, -ial, -ian, -ic, and -ical.*																			●	●	●	●	●	●
64	Recognize and use the suffixes -ative, -itive, and -ive, meaning "inclined to," to form an adjective: • -ative: e.g., affirm/affirmative, conserve/conservative, interpret/interpretative, authority/authoritative, tent/tentative • -itive: e.g., add/additive, compete/competitive, sens/sensitive • -ive: e.g., act/active, impulse/impulsive, pens/pensive	*Add the suffix -ative, -itive, or -ive to some nouns, verbs, or word roots to form adjectives.* *Add the suffix -ative, -itive, or -ive to the end of a word root base word to mean "inclined to."* *Use the basic rules to spell words correctly when adding the suffixes -ative, -itive, and -ive.* *Sometimes the suffixes -ative, -itive, and -ive require the use of additional spelling rules:* • *For some words that end with a y, drop the y and add -ative, -itive, or -ive.*																						●	●	●

Suffixes: Noun Suffixes

#	BEHAVIOR	INSTRUCTIONAL LANGUAGE	PreK E	PreK M	PreK L	K E	K M	K L	1 E	1 M	1 L	2 E	2 M	2 L	3 E	3 M	3 L	4 E	4 M	4 L	5 E	5 M	5 L	6	7	8
65	Recognize and use the suffixes *-er, -or, -ar,* and *-ist,* which name a person or thing that does something, to form a noun: • -er: e.g., *teach/teacher, bake/baker, drum/drummer, transmit/transmitter, develop/developer, carry/carrier, employ/employer, picnic/picnicker* • -or: e.g., *visit/visitor, operate/operator, bet/bettor, edit/editor, survey/surveyor* • -ar: e.g., *burgle/burglar, beg/beggar* • -ist: e.g., *art/artist, type/typist, drug/druggist, humor/humorist, essay/essayist, biology/biologist, piano/pianist*	Add the suffixes *-er, -or, -ar,* or *-ist* to the end of a base word to name a person or thing that does something. Use the basic rules to spell words correctly when adding the suffixes *-er, -or, -ar,* and *-ist.* Sometimes the suffixes *-er, -or, -ar,* and *-ist* require the use of additional spelling rules: • For words that end with hard c, add k before adding *-er.* • For some words that end with a consonant and y, drop the y and add *-ist.* • For some words that end with an o, drop the o and add *-ist.*										•	•	•	•	•	•	•								
66	Recognize and use the suffix *-ness,* meaning "state or quality of being," to form a noun: e.g., *kind/kindness, close/closeness, fit/fitness, bitter/bitterness, dizzy/dizziness*	Add the suffix *-ness* to the end of a base word to mean "state or quality of being." Use the basic rules to spell words correctly when adding the suffix *-ness.*																	•	•	•	•	•	•	•	•
67	Recognize and use the suffixes *-ion, -tion,* and *-sion,* to show the quality or state of something by changing a verb to a noun: • -ion: e.g., *adopt/adoption, commune/communion; discuss/discussion, revise/revision, create/creation, protect/protection* • -tion: e.g., *introduce/introduction* • -sion: e.g., *extend/extension, decide/decision*	Add the suffix *-ion, -tion,* or *-sion* to the end of a base word to show the quality or state of something. Use the basic rules to spell words correctly when adding the suffixes *-ion, -tion,* and *-sion.* When adding the suffixes *-ion, -tion,* and *-sion,* use the following rules to decide which suffix to add: • For words that end with ss, add *-ion.* • For words that end with se or te, drop the final e and add *-ion.* • For words that end with ct, add *-ion.* • For words that end with ce, drop the final e and add *-tion.* • For words that end with d or de, drop the d or de and add *-sion.*																	•	•	•	•	•	•	•	•

WORD STRUCTURE (continued)

BEHAVIOR	INSTRUCTIONAL LANGUAGE	PreK		K			1			2			3			4			5			6-8		
		E	M	E	M	L	E	M	L	E	M	L	E	M	L	E	M	L	E	M	L	6	7	8

Suffixes: Noun Suffixes (continued)

68 Recognize and use the suffix -ment, meaning "act of," "condition of being," or "product of," to form a noun: e.g., punish/punishment, measure/measurement, commit/commitment, employ/employment but argue/argument, merry/merriment.

Add the suffix -ment to the end of a word root or base word to mean "act of," "condition of being," or "product of."

For nearly all base words, there are no spelling changes when adding the suffix -ment. One exception is the word argument, *in which the e is dropped before the suffix -ment is added.*

Dots: 5 E, 5 M, 5 L, 6, 7, 8

69 Recognize and use the suffix -ity, meaning "state or condition of being," to form a noun: e.g., major/majority, dense/density, elastic/elasticity, complex/complexity.

Add the suffix -ity to the end of a base word to mean "state or condition of being."

Use the basic rules to spell words correctly when adding the suffix -ity.

Sometimes the suffix -ity requires the use of additional spelling rules:

- *For words that end with a single vowel and the consonant x, the x is not doubled before adding -ity*

Dots: 5 E, 5 M, 5 L, 6, 7, 8

70 Recognize and use the suffixes -ant and -ent, meaning "someone or something that performs an action," to form a noun:
- -ant: e.g., assist/assistant, pollute/pollutant, inhabit/inhabitant, occupy/occupant
- -ent: e.g., correspond/correspondent, reside/resident

Add the suffix -ant or -ent to the end of a base word to mean "someone or something that performs an action."

Use the basic rules to spell words correctly when adding the suffixes -ant and -ent.

One exception to the basic rules is the word occupant, *in which the y is dropped before the suffix -ant is added.*

Dots: 5 E, 5 M, 5 L, 6, 7, 8

71 Recognize and use the suffixes -ance and -ence, meaning "state of" or "quality of," to form a noun:
- -ance: e.g., attend/attendance, endure/endurance, admit/admittance, rely/reliance, annoy/annoyance
- -ence: e.g., exist/existence, coincide/coincidence, excel/excellence

Add the suffix -ance or -ence to the end of a base word to mean "state of" or "quality of."

Use the basic rules to spell words correctly when adding the suffixes -ance and -ence.

Dots: 5 E, 5 M, 5 L, 6, 7, 8

BEHAVIOR	INSTRUCTIONAL LANGUAGE	PreK			K			1			2			3			4			5			6-8		
		E	M	L	E	M	L	E	M	L	E	M	L	E	M	L	E	M	L	E	M	L	6	7	8

Suffixes: Noun Suffixes (continued)

72 Recognize and use the suffixes that mean "act or process of," "state of," "result of," "amount or collection of," or "something that" to form a noun:
- -age: e.g., *short/shortage, use/usage, bag/baggage, marry/marriage*
- -ure: e.g., *moist/moisture, legislate/legislature, fract/fracture*

Instructional Language:
Add the suffix -age or -ure to the end of word roots or base words to mean "act or process of," "state of," or "result of."
Add the suffix -age to the end of base words to mean "amount or collection of."
Add the suffix -ure to the end of word roots or base words to mean "something that."
Use the basic rules to spell words correctly when adding the suffixes -age and -ure.

Grade dots: 5 (E, M, L), 6, 7, 8

73 Recognize and use the suffixes -arium and -orium, meaning "a place for," to form a noun:
- -arium: e.g., *planetarium, solarium*
- -orium: e.g., *auditorium, emporium*

Instructional Language:
Use the suffix -arium or -orium, meaning "a place for," to form a noun.
Use the basic rules to spell words correctly when adding the suffixes -arium and -orium.

Grade dots: 5 (E, M, L), 6, 7, 8

Prefixes

74 Understand and discuss the concept of a prefix.

Instructional Language:
A prefix is a group of letters put at the beginning of a word root or base word to change its meaning.

Grade dots: 2 (M, L), 3 (E, M, L), 4 (E, M, L), 5 (E, M, L), 6, 7, 8

75 Recognize and use the prefix *re-*, meaning "again": e.g., *remake, repay, reassure, refresh.*

Instructional Language:
Add the prefix re- to the beginning of a word root or base word to mean "again."

Grade dots: 3 (E, M, L), 4 (E, M, L), 5 (E, M, L), 6, 7, 8

76 Recognize and use prefixes that mean "not": e.g.,
- un- *(unfair, unkind, unaware, unravel)*
- in- *(invisible, incredible, insane, infinite)*
- dis- *(disappear, dislike, disobey, disagree)*
- non- *(nonsense, nonfiction, nonstop, nonviolent)*

Instructional Language:
Add the prefix un- to the beginning of a word root or base word to mean "not" or "opposite of."
Add the prefix in- to the beginning of a word root or base word to mean "not."
Add the prefix dis- or non- to the beginning of a word root or base word to mean "not," "lack of," or "opposite of."

Grade dots: 2 (M, L), 3 (E, M, L), 4 (E, M, L), 5 (E, M, L), 6, 7, 8

77 Recognize and use prefixes that mean "bad, badly" or "wrong, wrongly": e.g.,
- mis- *(mistake, mislead, misfortune)*
- mal- *(malform, malfunction, malpractice)*

Instructional Language:
Add the prefix mis- or mal- to the beginning of a word root or base word to mean "bad, badly" or "wrong, wrongly."

Grade dots: 3 (E, M, L), 4 (E, M, L), 5 (E, M, L), 6, 7, 8

WORD STRUCTURE (side tab)

	BEHAVIOR	INSTRUCTIONAL LANGUAGE	PreK		K			1			2			3			4			5			6–8		
			E	M	E	M	L	E	M	L	E	M	L	E	M	L	E	M	L	E	M	L	6	7	8

Prefixes (continued)

78	Recognize and use prefixes that refer to sequence: e.g., • pre-, meaning "before" (preheat, precaution, predict, prescribe) • fore-, meaning "before," "earlier," or "in front" (forefather, forehead, foresee, foretell) • pro-, meaning "before" or "forward" (proactive, proclaim, promotion) • ante-, meaning "before" (antedate, anteroom, antechamber, antecedent) • post-, meaning "after" (postdate, postpone, postwar, postscript)	Add the prefix pre-, fore-, pro-, or ante- to the beginning of a word root or base word to mean "before." Add the prefix post- to the beginning of a word root base word to mean "after."													•	•	•	•	•	•	•	•	•	•	•
79	Recognize and use prefixes that indicate amount, extent, or location: e.g., • sub- (subway, submarine, subsoil, subset) • super- (supermarket, superpower, superscript, supernatural)	Add the prefix sub- to the beginning of a word root or base word to mean "under or lower" or "smaller." Add the prefix super- to the beginning of a word root or base word to mean "very large and powerful," "above," or "beyond."													•	•	•	•	•	•	•	•	•	•	•
80	Recognize and use number-related prefixes: e.g., uniform, monarch, monogram, bicycle, triangle, quadrangle, pentagon, octopus, decade, century, hemisphere, semicircle, multicolor, polyrhythmic.	Add the prefix uni-, mon-, or mono- to the beginning of a word to mean "one." Add the prefix bi- to the beginning of a word to mean "two." Add the prefix tri- to the beginning of a word to mean "three." Add the prefix quad- to the beginning of a word to mean "four." Add the prefix pent- to the beginning of a word to mean "five." Add the prefix oct- to the beginning of a word to mean "eight." Add the prefix dec- to the beginning of a word to mean "ten." Add the prefix cent- to the beginning of a word to mean "hundred." Add the prefix hemi- or semi- to the beginning of a word to mean "half." Add the prefix multi- or poly- to the beginning of a word to mean "many."																•	•	•	•	•	•	•	•	•

WORD STRUCTURE (continued)

BEHAVIOR	INSTRUCTIONAL LANGUAGE	PreK			K			1			2			3			4			5			6-8		
		E	M	L	E	M	L	E	M	L	E	M	L	E	M	L	E	M	L	E	M	L	6	7	8
Prefixes (continued)																									
81 Recognize and use prefixes that mean "with or together" or "between or among": e.g., • com- (compile, compose, compress) • con- (construct, confer, conform) • inter- (interact, interchange, interlock)	Add the prefix com- or con- to the beginning of a word to mean "with or together." Add the prefix inter- to the beginning of a word to mean "together" or "between or among."																•	•	•	•	•	•	•	•	•
82 Recognize and use prefixes that mean "out," "without," "from," or "away," or "in, into, or within": e.g., • ex- (explode, export, exclude) • in- (inspect, include, inflate) • intra- (intracompany, intrastate, intravenous)	Add the prefix ex- to the beginning of a word to mean "out," "without," "from," or "away." Add the prefix in- or intra- to the beginning of a word to mean "in, into, or within" or "inside."																•	•	•	•	•	•	•	•	•
83 Recognize and use prefixes that mean "make" or "put in or put on": e.g., • em- (empower, embed, embark) • en- (enclose, enable, entangle)	Add the prefix em- or en- to the beginning of a word to mean "make" or "put in or put on."																			•	•	•	•	•	•
84 Recognize and use prefixes that mean "around," "across," or "beyond," or "through": e.g., • circu-, circum- (circular, circuit, circumference) • peri- (periscope, perimeter, period) • trans- (transport, transaction, transatlantic) • per- (permit, perspiration, persist)	Add the prefix circu- or circum- to the beginning of a word to mean "around." Add the prefix peri- to the beginning of a word to mean "around" or "near." Add the prefix trans- to the beginning of a word to mean "across" or "beyond." Add the prefix per- to the beginning of a word to mean "beyond or through."																			•	•	•	•	•	•
85 Recognize and use prefixes that mean "opposite" or "against": e.g., • ant-, anti- (antonym, antacid, antifreeze, antisocial) • contra-, contro- (contradict, contraband, controversy, controversial) • counter- (counterclockwise, counterpart)	Add the prefix ant-, anti-, contra-, contro-, or counter- to the beginning of a word to mean "opposite" or "against."																			•	•	•	•	•	•

WORD STRUCTURE (continued)

	BEHAVIOR	INSTRUCTIONAL LANGUAGE	PreK			K			1			2			3			4			5			6-8		
			E	M	L	E	M	L	E	M	L	E	M	L	E	M	L	E	M	L	E	M	L	6	7	8

Prefixes (continued)

	BEHAVIOR	INSTRUCTIONAL LANGUAGE	PreK E	M	L	K E	M	L	1 E	M	L	2 E	M	L	3 E	M	L	4 E	M	L	5 E	M	L	6	7	8
86	Recognize and use the prefix *de-*, which means "opposite," "down or lower," or "take away or remove": e.g., *decentralize, depress, descend, defrost.*	Add the prefix de- to the beginning of a word root or base word to mean "opposite," "down or lower," or "take away or remove."																				•	•	•	•	•	•
87	Recognize and use prefixes that change form depending on the first letter of the word root or base word (assimilated prefixes): e.g., **in-** meaning "not" or "in, into, or within" *(invisibility, inability)* • il- *(illegal, illegible)* • im- *(immigrant, immortal)* • ir- *(irregular, irresponsible)* **ad-** meaning "to or toward" *(adjoin, adhere)* • ac- *(account, acclaim)* • af- *(affect, affirm)* • ag- *(aggressive, aggravate)* • al- *(allow, allot)* • an- *(announce, annex)* • ap- *(approach, approve)* • ar- *(arrest, arrival)* • as- *(assign, assure)* • at- *(attempt, attraction)* **sub-** meaning "under or lower" or "smaller" *(subtract, submarine)* • suc- *(success, succession)* • suf- *(suffix, sufficient)* • sug- *(suggestion)* • sum- *(summon)* • sup- *(suppose, suppress)* • sur- *(surround, surrender)* • sus- *(suspect, suspend)* **ob-** meaning "to," "toward," or "against" *(observe, obstruct)* • oc- *(occupy, occur)* • of- *(offer, offend)* • op- *(oppose, oppress)* • o- *(omit)* *(continues)*	Sometimes the spelling of a prefix changes depending on the first letter of the word root or base word. When in- is added to some word root or base words, the n is changed depending on the first letter in the word root or base word. Add the prefix in- for the assimilated prefixes il-, im-, and ir- to the beginning of a word root or base word to mean "not" or "in, into, or within." When ad- is added to some word root or base words, the d is changed depending on the first letter in the word root or base word. Add the prefix ad- for the assimilated prefixes ac-, af-, ag-, al-, an-, ap-, ar-, as-, and at- to the beginning of a word root or base word to mean "to or toward." When sub- is added to some word root or base words, the b is changed depending on the first letter in the word root or base word. Add the prefix sub- for the assimilated prefixes suc-, suf-, sug-, sum-, sup-, sur-, and sus- to the beginning of a word root or base word to mean "under or lower" or "smaller." When ob- is added to some word root or base words, the b is changed depending on the first letter in the word root or base word. Add the prefix ob- for the assimilated prefixes oc-, of-, op-, and o- to the beginning of a word root or base word to mean "to," "toward," or "against."																				•	•	•	•	•	•

BEHAVIOR	INSTRUCTIONAL LANGUAGE	GRADE LEVEL																						
		PreK			K			1			2			3			4			5			6-8		
		E	M	L	E	M	L	E	M	L	E	M	L	E	M	L	E	M	L	E	M	L	6	7	8

Prefixes (continued)

87 *(continued)*

com- meaning "with or together" *(companion, compact)*
- col- *(collide, collapse)*
- con- *(connect, connotation)*
- cor- *(correspond, corrode)*
- co- *(coordinate, coworker)*

ex- meaning "out," "without," "from," or "away" *(exclaim, exchange)*
- ef- *(effort, effective)*
- e- *(elapse, erase)*

When com- is added to some word root or base words, the m is changed depending on the first letter in the word root or base word. Add the prefix com- for the assimilated prefixes col-, con-, cor-, and co- to the beginning of a word root or base word to mean "with or together."

When ex- is added to some word root or base words, the x is changed depending on the first letter in the word root or base word. Add the prefix ex- for the assimilated prefixes ef- and e- to the beginning of a word root or base word to mean "out," "without," "from," or "away."

(Grade dots: 5 E, 5 M, 5 L, 6, 7, 8)

Abbreviations

88 Recognize and use common abbreviations and understand the full form of the words they shorten: e.g.,
- titles, names, degrees, and professional terms: *Mr.* (*Mister*, title for a man), *Ms.* (title for a woman), *Mrs.* (title for a married woman), *Miss* (title for a girl or an unmarried woman), *Dr.* (*Doctor*), *Sgt.* (*Sergeant*); *Jr.* (*Junior*), *Sr.* (*Senior*); *MD* or *M.D.* (*Doctor of Medicine*), *PhD* or *Ph.D.* (*Doctor of Philosophy*), *RN* or *R.N.* (*Registered Nurse*)
- days of week and months: *Mon.* (*Monday*), *Tues., Wed., Thurs., Fri., Sat., Sun.; Jan.* (*January*), *Feb., Mar., Apr., Aug., Sept., Oct., Nov., Dec*
- addresses and geographical terms: *St.* (*Street*), *Ave.* (*Avenue*), *Rd.* (*Road*), *Apt.* (*Apartment*), *Blvd.* (*Boulevard*), *CA* or *Calif.* (*California*), *U.S.* or *US* (*United States*); *Mt.* (*Mountain*), *E* (*East*), *N, W, S*

(continues)

Some words have a shortened form that uses some of the letters. They are abbreviations.

Abbreviations are usually pronounced the same as the longer form of the word.

Many abbreviations begin with an uppercase letter, and most are followed by a period.

(Grade dots: 2 E through 8)

WORD STRUCTURE

WORD STRUCTURE (continued)

BEHAVIOR	INSTRUCTIONAL LANGUAGE	GRADE LEVEL																							
		PreK			K			1			2			3			4			5			6-8		
		E	M	L	E	M	L	E	M	L	E	M	L	E	M	L	E	M	L	E	M	L	6	7	8

Abbreviations (continued)

88 (continued) • scholarly references: *etc.* (*et cetera*), *e.g.* (*for example*), *i.e.* (*that is*), *p.* (*page*), *pp.* (*pages*), *ed.* (*edition* or *editor*), *vol.* (*volume*), *fig.* (*figure*) • times and dates: *a.m.* or AM (*the time from midnight to noon*), *p.m.* or PM (*the time from noon to midnight*); *BCE* or *B.C.E.* (*before the Common Era*), *CE* or *C.E.* (*of the Common Era*) • measurements: *in.* (*inch or inches*), *ft.* (*foot or feet*), *yd.* (*yard or yards*), *mi.* (*mile or miles*), *lb.* (*pound or pounds*), *oz.* (*ounce or ounces*), *c* or *c.* (*cup or cups*), *pt.* (*pint or pints*), *qt.* (*quart or quarts*), *gal.* (*gallon or gallons*), *cu.* or *cu* (*cubic*), *sq.* (*square*), *mph* or *m.p.h.* (*miles per hour*); *mm* (*millimeter or millimeters*), *mg* (*milligram or milligrams*), *ml* (*milliliter or milliliters*), *cm* (*centimeter or centimeters*), *km* (*kilometer or kilometers*) • businesses and organizations: *Co.* (*Company*), *Corp.* (*Corporation*), *Inc.* (*Incorporated*), *Ltd.* (*Limited*), *Assoc.* or *Assn.* (*Association*), *dept.* (*department*), *asst.* or *Asst.* (*assistant*), *pd.* (*paid*)	Some words have a shortened form that uses some of the letters. They are abbreviations. Abbreviations are usually pronounced the same as the longer form of the word. Many abbreviations begin with an uppercase letter, and most are followed by a period.													•	•	•	•	•	•	•	•	•	•	•	•

	BEHAVIOR	INSTRUCTIONAL LANGUAGE	GRADE LEVEL																							
			PreK			K			1			2			3			4			5			6-8		
			E	M	L	E	M	L	E	M	L	E	M	L	E	M	L	E	M	L	E	M	L	6	7	8
Word Roots																										
89	Recognize and use word roots from Latin or Greek: • Latin–e.g., *aqua, aud, bene, cap, centr, clos, clud, clus, corp, cred, dict, duc, duct, dur, equa, equi, fac, fer, fic, fin, firm, flect, flex, form, fract, frag, grad, gress, hab, hib, ject, join, junct, loc, luc, lum, man, mem, min, miss, mit, mob, mot, mov, ped, pel, pend, pens, pon, pop, port, pos, prim, prin, pub, puls, quer, ques, quir, quis, rupt, scribe, script, sens, sent, sign, sist, sol, son, spec, sta, stat, stit, stru, struct, tain, tempo, ten, tent, tin, terr, tract, val, ven, vent, ver, vers, vert, vid, vis, voc, vok* • Greek–e.g., *aer, arch, aster, astr, astro, bio, chron, cycl, dem, geo, gram, graph, hydr, hydro, log, mega, meter, micro, ology, phon, photo, pod, pol, poli, polis, scop, scope, tele, therm*	*Many words and parts of words come from ancient languages called Greek and Latin. Use Greek and Latin roots to help you learn the meanings of words.*																	•	•	•	•	•	•	•	•	•

Word-Solving Actions

Word-Solving Actions

Word-solving actions are the strategic moves readers and writers make when they use their knowledge of the language system to solve words. These strategies are "in-the-head" actions that are invisible, although we can often infer them from overt behaviors. The principles listed in this category of learning represent students' ability to use the principles in all previous categories of this section of *The Fountas & Pinnell Literacy Continuum*.

Classroom lessons developed around these principles should provide opportunities for students to apply concepts in active ways—for example, through sorting, building, locating, reading, or writing. Lessons related to word-solving actions demonstrate to them how they can problem-solve by working on words in isolation or while reading or writing continuous text. The more they can integrate these strategies into their reading and writing systems, the more flexible they will become in solving words. The reader/writer may use knowledge of letter-sound relationships, for example, either to solve an unfamiliar word or to check that the reading is accurate. Knowledge of word parts and patterns, ability to connect words, access to the meaning of base words and affixes, knowledge of the meaning of roots—all are tools in the process. Rapid, automatic word solving is a basic component of fluency and important for comprehension because it frees children's attention to focus on the meaning and language of the text.

WORD-SOLVING ACTIONS

	BEHAVIOR	INSTRUCTIONAL LANGUAGE	PreK E	PreK M	PreK L	K E	K M	K L	1 E	1 M	1 L	2 E	2 M	2 L	3 E	3 M	3 L	4 E	4 M	4 L	5 E	5 M	5 L	6	7	8
	Using What Is Known to Solve Words																									
1	Recognize and find names.	*A person's name starts with a capital letter. The other letters are lowercase.* *Knowing the first letter in a person's name can help you find the name in print.*	•	•	•	•	•	•	•																	
2	Use the initial letter in a name to make connections to other words: e.g., *Max, Maria, make, home, from*.	*Connect a name with other words.* *The first letter in a name is the same as the first letter in some other names.* *The first letter in a name is the same as the first letter in some other words.* *The first letter in a name can be found in some other words.*	•	•	•	•	•	•	•																	
3	Use the letters in names to make connections to other words: e.g., *Dan, money, run*.	*Any letter in a name can be found in some other words.*	•	•	•	•	•	•	•																	

		GRADE LEVEL																							
BEHAVIOR	**INSTRUCTIONAL LANGUAGE**	PreK			K			1			2			3			4			5			6-8		
		E	M	L	E	M	L	E	M	L	E	M	L	E	M	L	E	M	L	E	M	L	6	7	8
Using What Is Known to Solve Words *(continued)*																									
4 Use the initial letter in a name to read and write other words: e.g., *T*om, *t*oy, *t*own, *st*op, *c*at.	*Connect a name with other words you want to read.* *Connect the first letter in a name with the first letter in another word you want to read.* *Connect the first letter in a name with that same letter found in another word you want to read.* *Connect a name with other words you want to write.* *Connect the first letter in a name with the first letter in another word you want to write.* *Connect the first letter in a name with that same letter found in another word you want to write.*					•	•	•	•	•	•	•														
5 Use the letters in names to read and write other words: e.g., *M*eg, be*g*an, bi*g*.	*Connect any letter in a name with that same letter found in another word you want to read.* *Connect any letter in a name with that same letter found in another word you want to write.*				•	•	•	•	•	•																
6 Identify rhyming words and use them to solve unknown words: e.g., *down/clown/drown.*	*Connect an unknown word with a rhyming word to solve the unknown word.*							•	•	•	•	•	•	•											
7 Use known words to monitor word-solving accuracy.	*Use words you know to check your reading.*					•	•	•	•	•	•	•														
8 Recognize and read known words quickly.	*When you know a word, you can read the word quickly.*							•	•	•	•	•	•	•	•	•	•	•								
9 Use knowledge of letter-sound relationships to monitor word-solving accuracy.	*Use what you know about letters and sounds to check your reading.*							•	•	•	•	•	•	•	•	•	•	•								
10 Identify words that start the same and use them to solve unknown words: e.g., *b*at, *b*ell.	*Words can start with the same sound and letter.* *Connect words that start with the same sound and letter.*					•	•	•	•	•	•															
11 Use onsets and rimes in known words to read and write other words with the same parts: e.g., *thr*-ow, *thr*-ee; th*r-ow*, g*r-ow*.	*Sometimes a part of a word you know can be found in another word.* *Use parts of words you know to read or write another word with the same parts.*								•	•	•	•	•	•	•	•	•									
12 Identify words that end the same and use them to solve unknown words: e.g., chi*n*, mai*n*.	*Words can end with the same sound and letter.* *Connect words that end with the same sound and letter.*									•	•	•	•	•	•	•										

WORD-SOLVING ACTIONS

WORD-SOLVING ACTIONS (continued)

	BEHAVIOR	INSTRUCTIONAL LANGUAGE	PreK		K			1			2			3			4			5			6-8		
			E	M	E	M	L	E	M	L	E	M	L	E	M	L	E	M	L	E	M	L	6	7	8

Using What Is Known to Solve Words (continued)

| 13 | Identify words that have the same letter pattern and use them to solve an unknown word: e.g., *hat/sat, light/night, crumb/thumb, curious/furious.* | Some words have parts (patterns) that are the same.

Patterns (parts) that are the same appear in many words.

Look at and use the familiar pattern (part) to read a word. | | | | | | • | • | • | • | • | • | • | • | • | • | • | • | • | • | | | | | |
| 14 | Use known word parts (some are words) to solve unknown larger words: e.g., <u>in</u>/<u>in</u>to, <u>can</u>, <u>can</u>vas; <u>us</u>, cr<u>ust</u>. | Use words you know to read some longer words. | | | | | | | • | • | • | • | • | • | • | • | • | • | • | • | | | | | |

Analyzing Words to Solve Them

15	Say a word slowly to hear the initial sound in the word.	Saying a word slowly makes it easier to hear the first sound in the word.	•	•	•	•	•	•	•	•															
16	Say a word slowly to hear the final sound in the word.	Saying a word slowly makes it easier to hear the last sound in the word.	•	•	•	•	•	•	•	•															
17	Say a word slowly to hear the sounds in sequence.	Saying a word slowly makes it easier to hear each sound in order from first to last.						•	•	•	•	•													
18	Recognize the sequence of letters and the sequence of sounds to read a word or word part.	Read a word by looking at each letter from left to right and by thinking about each sound in order. Thinking about the order of the letters and sounds is a way of solving an unknown word.							•	•	•	•	•	•	•	•									
19	Recognize and use onsets and rimes to read words: e.g., *b-ag, bag; gr-in, grin; pl-ate, plate.*	Look at the first part and the last part of a word to read the word. Use parts of words you know to read an unknown word.						•	•	•	•	•	•	•	•	•	•								

Changing, Adding, or Removing Parts to Solve Words

| 20 | Change the beginning sound or sounds to make and solve a new word: e.g., *he/me* (change /h/ to /m/), *more/shore* (change /m/ to /sh/), *bright/might* (change /b/ /r/ to /m/). | Change the first sound or sounds in a word to make another word. | | | | | | • | • | • | • | • | • | • | • | | | | | | | | | | |
| 21 | Change the ending sound or sounds to make and solve a new word: e.g., *in/it* (change /n/ to /t/), *them/then* (change /m/ to /n/), *rest/red* (change /s/ /t/ to /d/). | Change the last sound or sounds in a word to make another word. | | | | | | | • | • | • | • | • | • | • | | | | | | | | | | |

The Fountas & Pinnell Comprehensive Phonics, Spelling, and Word Study Guide

WORD-SOLVING ACTIONS

BEHAVIOR	INSTRUCTIONAL LANGUAGE	GRADE LEVEL																						
		PreK			K			1			2			3			4			5			6-8		
		E	M	L	E	M	L	E	M	L	E	M	L	E	M	L	E	M	L	E	M	L	6	7	8
Changing, Adding, or Removing Parts to Solve Words (continued)																									
22 Change a middle sound to make and solve a new word: e.g., *big/bag* (change /i/ to /a/), *fill/fell* (change /i/ to /e/), *bank/bunk* (change /a/ to /u/).	Change a middle sound in a word to make another word.										•	•	•	•	•	•									
23 Change an onset or rime to read or write other words: e.g., *br-ing*, *th-ing* (change *br* to *th*), *br-ing*, *br-own* (change *ing* to *own*).	Change the first part or the last part of a word to read or write another word.										•	•	•	•	•	•	•								
24 Add a letter to the beginning or end of a word to read and write other words: e.g., *in/win; ten/tent; for/fork.*	Add a letter to the beginning of a word to read or write another word. Add a letter to the end of a word to read or write another word.										•	•	•	•	•	•	•								
25 Add a consonant cluster or a consonant digraph to the beginning or end of a word to read and write other words: e.g., *an/plan, in/thin; go/gold, tea/teach.*	A group of two or three consonant letters is a consonant cluster or a consonant digraph. In a consonant cluster, you hear the sound of each consonant. In a consonant digraph, you a hear a single unique sound. Add a consonant cluster or a consonant digraph to the beginning of a word to read or write another word. Add a consonant cluster or a consonant digraph to the end of a word to read or write another word.											•	•	•	•	•	•								
26 Remove a letter from the beginning or end of a word to read and write other words: e.g., *sit/it, his/is; bark/bar.*	Read the word and say it aloud. Remove the first letter of the word. Read or write the new word. Read the word and say it aloud. Remove the last letter of the word. Read or write the new word.											•	•	•	•	•	•								
27 Remove a consonant cluster or a consonant digraph from the beginning or end of a word to read and write other words: e.g., *plan/an, thin/in; gold/go, teach/tea.*	A group of two or three consonant letters is a consonant cluster or a consonant digraph. In a consonant cluster, you hear the sound of each consonant. In a consonant digraph, you a hear a single unique sound. Read the word and say it aloud. Remove the beginning consonant cluster or consonant digraph. Read or write the new word. Read the word and say it aloud. Remove the ending consonant cluster or consonant digraph. Read or write the new word.											•	•	•	•	•	•								
28 Remove the inflectional ending from a base word to read and write other words: e.g., *sits/sit, jumping/jump, player/play, wished/wish.*	Remove the ending from some words to read or write other words.										•	•	•	•											

WORD-SOLVING ACTIONS

WORD-SOLVING ACTIONS *(continued)*

	BEHAVIOR	INSTRUCTIONAL LANGUAGE	PreK E	PreK M	PreK L	K E	K M	K L	1 E	1 M	1 L	2 E	2 M	2 L	3 E	3 M	3 L	4 E	4 M	4 L	5 E	5 M	5 L	6	7	8
	**Taking Words Apart to Solve Them**																									
29	Take apart a compound word to read two smaller words: e.g., *birthday, birth, day; everywhere, every, where; sidewalk, side, walk.*	Some words are made of two smaller words and are called compound words. Dividing a compound word into two smaller words makes the compound word easier to read.									●	●	●	●	●	●	●									
30	Break a word into syllables to decode manageable units: e.g., *re/mem/ber, hos/pi/tal, be/fore, de/part/ment.*	You can listen for the syllables in words. Some words have one syllable. Some words have more than one syllable. Each syllable in a word has a vowel sound. You can break a word into syllables. Look at the syllables in a word to read it.									●	●	●	●	●	●	●	●	●	●	●	●	●	●	●	●
	**Using Strategies to Solve Words and Determine Their Meanings**																									
31	Use connections between or among words that mean the same or almost the same to solve an unknown word: e.g., *damp, wet.*	Some words mean the same. They are synonyms. Think about words with similar meanings. Use a connection between an unknown word and a word you know that has a similar meaning to help solve the unknown word.								●	●	●	●	●	●	●	●	●	●	●	●	●	●			
32	Use connections between or among words that mean the opposite or almost the opposite to solve an unknown word: e.g., *stale, fresh.*	Some words have opposite meanings. They are antonyms. Think about words with opposite or nearly opposite meanings. Use a connection between an unknown word and a word you know that has an opposite meaning to help solve the unknown word.								●	●	●	●	●	●	●	●	●	●	●	●	●				
33	Recognize and use word parts to solve an unknown word and understand its meaning: e.g., *conference*–prefix *con-* ("with or together"), Latin root *fer* ("to bring" or "to carry"), suffix *-ence* ("state of" or "quality of").	An unknown word may contain one or more word parts–word root, base word, prefix, or suffix. Any word root, base word, or affix may contain hints about the meaning of an unknown word.															●	●	●	●	●	●	●	●	●	●
34	Recognize and use connections between or among related words that have the same word root or base word to solve unknown words: e.g., *support/supports/supported/supportive/unsupportive.*	Connect words that have the same word root or base word but different prefixes and/or suffixes to solve unknown words. These words have different but related meanings.																	●	●	●	●	●	●	●	●
35	Recognize and use a word's origin to solve an unknown word and understand its form and meaning.	The history of a word is its etymology. Knowing the origin of a word can help in solving it and understanding its form and meaning.																			●	●	●	●	●	●

The Fountas & Pinnell Comprehensive Phonics, Spelling, and Word Study Guide

	BEHAVIOR	INSTRUCTIONAL LANGUAGE	PreK			K			1			2			3			4			5			6–8		
			E	M	L	E	M	L	E	M	L	E	M	L	E	M	L	E	M	L	E	M	L	6	7	8
Using Strategies to Solve Words and Determine Their Meanings *(continued)*																										
36	Recognize and use Latin roots to solve an unknown word and determine its meaning: e.g., the Latin root *cred*, meaning "believe," in the word *credible*, meaning "capable of being believed" or "believable."	Many words come from Latin. They have Latin roots. A Latin root may contain hints about the meaning of an unfamiliar word.																		•	•	•	•	•	•	•
37	Recognize and use Greek roots to solve an unknown word and determine its meaning: e.g., the Greek root *graph*, meaning "write" in the word *autograph*, meaning "the writing of one's name."	Many words come from Greek. They have Greek roots. A Greek root may contain hints about the meaning of an unfamiliar word.																		•	•	•	•	•	•	•
Using Reference Tools to Solve and Find Information About Words																										
38	Use alphabetical order to locate information about words in a variety of reference tools.	Common reference tools with information about words include glossaries, dictionaries, and thesauruses. Information in most reference tools is arranged in alphabetical order. Use alphabetical order to find information in a glossary, dictionary, or other reference tool. Words that appear at the top of a page in some printed reference tools identify the first and last words on that page. They are guide words. Guide words make it easier to find a word quickly in an alphabetized reference tool.										•	•	•	•	•	•											
39	Use a glossary to solve and find information about words.	A glossary is a list of special or difficult words with explanations or comments. It is found at the end of a book. A glossary entry usually gives information about the spelling of a word and its meaning or meanings. Entries in a glossary are arranged in alphabetical order.										•	•	•	•	•	•	•	•	•	•	•	•	•	•	•	•	•
40	Use a dictionary to solve and find information about words.	A dictionary is a book or digital tool that contains information about the words of a language or of some special subject. A dictionary entry gives different types of information about a word, such as a word's spelling, syllables, pronunciation, meaning or meanings, as well as its history. Entries in a dictionary are arranged in alphabetical order.										•	•	•	•	•	•	•	•	•	•	•	•	•	•	•	•	•

WORD-SOLVING ACTIONS

WORD-SOLVING ACTIONS (continued)

#	BEHAVIOR	INSTRUCTIONAL LANGUAGE	PreK E	PreK M	PreK L	K E	K M	K L	1 E	1 M	1 L	2 E	2 M	2 L	3 E	3 M	3 L	4 E	4 M	4 L	5 E	5 M	5 L	6	7	8
	Using Reference Tools to Solve and Find Information About Words (continued)																									
41	Recognize and use different types of dictionaries (e.g., medical, foreign language, geographical, visual, reverse, thesaurus) to solve and find information about words.	Different types of dictionaries contain special kinds of information about words.																			•	•	•	•	•	•
	Spelling Strategies																									
42	Spell known words quickly.	When you know a word, you can spell the word quickly.				•	•	•	•	•	•	•	•	•	•	•										
43	Make a first attempt to spell an unknown word.	Try writing a word, and see if the spelling looks right.							•	•	•	•	•	•	•	•	•	•	•	•	•	•	•	•	•	•
44	Use known words to help spell an unknown word.	Use words you know to spell words you don't know.				•	•	•	•	•	•	•														
45	Use letter-sound relationships to help spell an unknown word.	Use what you know about letters and sounds to spell words you don't know.							•	•	•	•	•	•	•	•										
46	Use phonogram patterns and letter patterns to help spell a word.	Listen for the patterns of sounds and look for the patterns of letters in a word to spell the word.										•	•	•	•	•	•	•	•	•	•	•	•	•	•	•
47	Use sound and letter sequence to help spell a word.	Listen for each sound in a word and write the letter or letters that represent the sound in sequence.										•	•	•	•	•	•	•	•	•	•	•	•	•	•	•
48	Use syllables to help spell a word.	Listen for the sounds in each syllable in a word and write the letters that represent those sounds in sequence.													•	•	•	•	•	•	•	•	•	•	•	•
49	Use the spelling of the smaller words within a compound word to help spell a compound word.	Some words are made of two smaller words and are called compound words. See and use the spelling of each word part to spell a compound word.													•	•	•	•	•	•	•	•	•	•	•	•
50	Use a spelling routine to help spell a word.	Several routines can help in spelling words. One routine for spelling words is Choose, Write, Build, Mix, Fix, Mix. Another routine for spelling words is Look, Say, Cover, Write, Check. Another routine for spelling words is Buddy Check.													•	•	•	•	•	•	•	•	•	•	•	•
51	Use a mnemonic device to help spell a word: e.g., _friends_ to the _end_, a _bear_ bit my _ear_.	Make up a phrase or rhyme to help you spell a tricky word.													•	•	•	•	•	•	•	•	•	•	•	•

WORD-SOLVING ACTIONS

WORD-SOLVING ACTIONS (continued)

BEHAVIOR	INSTRUCTIONAL LANGUAGE	GRADE LEVEL																						
		PreK			K			1			2			3			4			5			6–8		
		E	M	L	E	M	L	E	M	L	E	M	L	E	M	L	E	M	L	E	M	L	6	7	8

Spelling Strategies *(continued)*

52 Use a dictionary to confirm or correct the spelling of a word.	*Check the spelling of a word by looking it up in a dictionary.* *Use a dictionary to correct a misspelled word.*													•	•	•	•	•	•	•	•	•	•	•	•
53 Use word origins to understand and remember the spelling of some words: e.g., *beret, chalet, champagne, lasagna, coyote, mosquito.*	*Sometimes you can figure out the spelling of a word by thinking about whether the word was added from another language and how that origin might affect the spelling.*														•	•	•	•	•	•	•	•	•	•	•
54 Use an electronic program to check your spelling.	*An electronic program can be helpful to check spelling.*																•	•	•	•	•	•	•	•	•
55 Ask for help when all known spelling strategies have been tried.	*When you have tried all of the strategies you know, ask for help spelling a word.*										•	•	•	•	•	•	•	•	•	•	•	•	•	•	•

Glossary

Glossary

abbreviation Shortened form of a word that uses some of the letters: e.g., *Mr., etc., NY.*

accented syllable A syllable that is given emphasis in pronunciation. See also *syllable, stress.*

acronym A word formed by combining the initial letter or letters of a group of words: e.g., *radar = ra*dio *detecting and ranging.*

adjective suffix A suffix put at the end of a word root or base word to form an adjective. See also *suffix.*

adjusting (as a strategic action) Reading in different ways as appropriate to the purpose for reading and type of text.

adverb suffix A suffix put at the end of a word root or base word to form an adverb. See also *suffix.*

affix A letter or group of letters added to the beginning or ending of a base or root word to change its meaning or function (a *prefix* or a *suffix*).

alphabet linking chart A chart containing upper- and lowercase letters of the alphabet paired with pictures representing words beginning with each letter (*a, apple*).

alphabetic principle The concept that there is a relationship between the spoken sounds in oral language and the graphic forms in written language.

analogy The resemblance of a known word to an unknown word that helps you solve the unknown word's meaning. Often an analogy shows the relationship between two pairs of words.

antonym A word that has the opposite meaning from another word: e.g., *cold* versus *hot.*

archaic word A word that is part of the language of the past and has specialized uses in language today.

assessment A means for gathering information or data that reveals what learners control, partially control, or do not yet control consistently.

automaticity Rapid, accurate, fluent word decoding without conscious effort or attention.

base word A word in its simplest form, which can be modified by adding affixes: e.g., *read; reread, reading.* A base word has meaning, can stand on its own, and is easily apparent in the language. Compare to *word root.*

behavior An observable action.

blend To combine sounds or word parts.

capitalization The use of capital letters, usually the first letter in a word, as a convention of written language (for example, for proper names and to begin sentences).

clipped word A word formed from shortening another word: e.g., *ad (advertisement).*

closed syllable A syllable that ends in a consonant: e.g., *lem*-on.

cognates Words that appear in different languages with very similar spellings and meanings.

comparative ending A suffix (e.g., *-er, -est*) put at the end of a base word to show comparison between or among two or more things.

compound word A word made of two or more smaller words or morphemes: e.g., *play ground.* The meaning of a compound word can be a combination of the meanings of the words it is made of or can be unrelated to the meanings of the combined units.

concept word A word that represents an abstract idea or name. Categories of concept words include color names, number words, days of the week, months of the year, seasons, and so on.

connotation The emotional meaning or association a word carries beyond its strict dictionary definition.

consonant A speech sound made by partial or complete closure of the airflow that causes friction at one or more points in the breath channel. The consonant sounds are represented by the letters *b, c, d, f, g, h, j, k, l, m, n, p, qu, r, s, t, v, w, y,* and *z.*

consonant blend Two or more consonant letters that often appear together in words and represent sounds that are smoothly joined, although each of the sounds can be heard in the word: e.g., *tr*im.

consonant cluster A sequence of two or three consonant letters: e.g., *tr*im, *ch*air.

consonant cluster linking charts Charts of common consonant clusters paired with pictures representing words beginning, or ending with each: e.g., *bl, block; sk, desk.*

consonant digraph Two consonant letters that appear together and represent a single sound that is different from the sound of either letter: e.g., sh*ell*.

contraction A shortened form of one or more words. A letter or letters are left out, and an apostrophe takes the place of the missing letter or letters.

cursive A form of handwriting in which letters are connected.

decoding Using letter-sound relationships to translate a word from a series of symbols to a unit of meaning.

diction Clear pronunciation and enunciation in speech.

directionality The orientation of print (in the English language, from left to right).

distinctive letter features Visual features that make each letter of the alphabet different from every other letter.

early literacy concepts Very early understandings related to how written language or print is organized and used—how it works.

English language learner A person whose native language is not English and who is acquiring English as an additional language.

fluency In reading, this term names the ability to read continuous text with good momentum, phrasing, appropriate pausing, intonation, and stress. In word solving, this term names the ability to solve words with speed, accuracy, and flexibility.

grapheme A letter or cluster of letters representing a single sound, or phoneme: e.g., *a, eigh, ay.*

graphophonic relationship The relationship between the oral sounds of the language and the written letters or clusters of letters. See also *semantic system, syntactic system.*

Greek root A word root that comes from Greek. Many English words contain Greek roots. See also *word root.*

high-frequency words Words that occur often in the spoken and written language.

homograph One of two or more words spelled alike but different in meaning, derivation, or pronunciation: e.g., the *bat* flew away, he swung the *bat;* take a *bow, bow* and arrow.

homonym One of two or more words spelled and pronounced alike but different in meaning: e.g., we had *quail* for dinner; I would *quail* in fear. A homonym is a type of homograph.

homophone One of two or more words pronounced alike but different in spelling and meaning: e.g., *meat, meet; bear, bare.*

idiom A phrase with meaning that cannot be derived from the conjoined meanings of its elements: e.g., *raining cats and dogs.*

inflectional ending A suffix added to a base word to show tense, plurality, possession, or comparison: e.g., dark-*er.*

intonation The rise and fall in pitch of the voice in speech to convey meaning.

language structure See *syntax.*

Latin root A word root that comes from Latin. Many English words contain Latin roots. See also *word root.*

letter combination Two or more letters that appear together and represent vowel sounds in words: e.g., *ea* in *meat, igh* in *sight.*

letter knowledge The ability to recognize and label the graphic symbols of language.

letters Graphic symbols representing the sounds in a language. Each letter has particular distinctive features and may be identified by letter name or sound.

letter-sound relationships The correspondence of letter(s) and sound(s) in written or spoken language.

lexicon Words that make up language.

long vowel The elongated vowel sound that is the same as the name of the vowel. It is sometimes represented by two or more letters: e.g., c*a*ke, *ei*ght, m*ai*l. Another term for long vowel is *lax vowel*.

lowercase letter A small letter form that is usually different from its corresponding capital or uppercase form.

monitoring (as a strategic action) Checking whether the reading sounds right, looks right, and makes sense.

morpheme The smallest unit of meaning in a language. Morphemes may be free or bound. For example, *run* is a unit of meaning that can stand alone (a free morpheme). In *runs* and *running*, the added *-s* and *-ing* are also units of meaning. They cannot stand alone but add meaning to the free morpheme. The *-s* and *-ing* are examples of bound morphemes.

morphemic strategies Ways of solving words by discovering meaning through the combination of significant word parts or morphemes: e.g., *happy, happiest; run, runner, running.*

morphological system Rules by which morphemes (building blocks of vocabulary) fit together into meaningful words, phrases, and sentences.

morphology The combination of morphemes (building blocks of meaning) to form words; the rules by which words are formed from free and bound morphemes—for example, root words, prefixes, and suffixes.

multiple-meaning word A word that means something different depending on the way it is used: e.g., *run—home run, run in your stocking, run down the street, a run of bad luck.*

multisyllable word A word that contains more than one syllable.

noun suffix A suffix put at the end of a word root or base word to form a noun. See also *suffix*.

onset In a syllable, the part (consonant, consonant cluster, or consonant digraph) that comes before the vowel: e.g., the *cr* in *cream*. See also *rime*.

onset-rime segmentation The identification and separation of the onset (first part) and rime (last part, containing the vowel) in a word: e.g., *dr-ip*.

open syllable A syllable that ends in a vowel sound: e.g., *ho*-tel.

orthographic awareness The knowledge of the visual features of written language, including distinctive features of letters as well as spelling patterns in words.

orthography The representation of the sounds of a language with the proper letters according to standard usage (spelling).

palindrome A word that is spelled the same in either direction: e.g., *noon*.

phoneme The smallest unit of sound in spoken language. There are forty-four units of speech sounds in English.

phoneme addition To add a beginning or ending sound to a word: e.g., /h/ + *and*; *an* + /t/.

phoneme blending To identify individual sounds and then to put them together smoothly to make a word: e.g., /k//a//t/ = *cat*.

phoneme deletion To omit a beginning, middle, or ending sound of a word: e.g., /k//a//s//k/ - /k/ = *ask*.

phoneme-grapheme correspondence The relationship between the sounds (phonemes) and letters (graphemes) of a language.

phoneme isolation The identification of an individual sound— beginning, middle, or end—in a word.

phoneme manipulation The movement of sounds from one place in a word to another.

phoneme reversal The exchange of the first and last sounds of a word to make a different word.

phoneme substitution The replacement of the beginning, middle, or ending sound of a word with a new sound.

phonemic (or phoneme) awareness The ability to hear individual sounds in words and to identify particular sounds.

phonemic strategies Ways of solving words that use how words sound and relationships between letters and letter clusters and phonemes in those words.

phonetics The scientific study of speech sounds—how the

sounds are made vocally and the relation of speech sounds to the total language process.

phonics The knowledge of letter-sound relationships and how they are used in reading and writing. Teaching phonics refers to helping children acquire this body of knowledge about the oral and written language systems; additionally, teaching phonics helps children use phonics knowledge as part of a reading and writing process. Phonics instruction uses a small portion of the body of knowledge that makes up phonetics.

phonogram A phonetic element represented by graphic characters or symbols. In word recognition, words containing a graphic sequence composed of a vowel grapheme and an ending consonant grapheme (such as *an* or *it*) are sometimes called a word family.

phonological awareness The awareness of words, rhyming words, onsets and rimes, syllables, and individual sounds (phonemes).

phonological system The sounds of the language and how they work together in ways that are meaningful to the speakers of the language.

plural Of, relating to, or constituting more than one.

possessive Grammatical form used to show ownership; e.g., *John's, his.*

prefix A group of letters placed in front of a base word to change its meaning: e.g., *pre*plan.

principle In phonics, a generalization or a sound-spelling relationship that is predictable.

***r*-controlled vowel sound** The modified or *r*-influenced sound of a vowel when it is followed by *r* in a syllable: e.g., *hurt.*

related words Words that are related because of sound, spelling, category, or meaning. See also *synonym, antonym, homophone, homograph, analogy.*

rhyme The repetition of vowel and consonant sounds in the stressed syllables of words in verse, especially at the ends of lines.

rime In a syllable, the ending part containing the letters that represent the vowel sound and the consonant letters that follow: i.e., dr-*eam.* See also *onset.*

schwa The sound of the middle vowel in an unstressed syllable (the *e* in *happen* and the sound between the *k* and *l* in *freckle*).

searching for and using information (as a strategic action) Finding and using meaning, language, or print information.

segment To divide into parts: e.g., *to/ma/to.*

self-correcting Noticing when reading doesn't make sense, sound right, or look right, and fixing it when it doesn't.

semantic system The system by which speakers of a language communicate meaning through

language. See also *graphophonic relationship, syntactic system.*

sets and subsets In relation to concept words, words that represent big ideas or items and words that represent related smaller ideas or items.

short vowel A brief-duration sound represented by a vowel letter: e.g., the |a| in *cat.*

silent *e* The final *e* in a spelling pattern that usually signals a long vowel sound in the word and that does not represent a sound itself: e.g., *make.*

solving words (as a strategic action) Using a range of strategies to take words apart and understand their meaning(s).

spelling patterns Beginning letters (onsets) and common phonograms (rimes), which form the basis for the English syllable. Knowing these patterns, a student can build countless words.

strategic action Any one of many simultaneous, coordinated thinking activities that go on in a reader's head. See *thinking within, beyond, and about the text.*

stress The emphasis given to some syllables or words in pronunciation. See also *accented syllable.*

suffix A group of letters added at the end of a base word or word root to change its function or meaning: e.g., hand*ful*, hope*less.*

summarizing (as a strategic action) Putting together and remembering important information, disregarding irrelevant information, while reading.

syllabication The division of words into syllables.

syllable A minimal unit of sequential speech sounds composed of a vowel sound or a consonant-vowel combination. A syllable always contains a vowel or vowel-like speech sound: e.g., *pen/ny*.

synonym One of two or more words that have different sounds but the same meaning: e.g., *high, tall*.

syntactic awareness The knowledge of grammatical patterns or structures.

syntactic system Rules that govern the ways in which morphemes and words work together in sentence patterns. This system is not the same as proper grammar, which refers to the accepted grammatical conventions. See also *graphophonic relationship, semantic system*.

syntax The way sentences are formed with words and phrases and the grammatical rules that govern their formation.

understandings Basic concepts that are critical to comprehending a particular area of content.

verb suffix A suffix put at the end of a word root or base word to form a verb. See also *suffix*.

visual processing Ways of solving words using knowledge of how words look, including the clusters and patterns of the letters in words.

vocabulary Words and their meanings. See also *word meaning / vocabulary*.

vowel A speech sound or phoneme made without stoppage of or friction in the airflow. The vowel sounds are represented by *a, e, i, o, u,* and sometimes *y*.

vowel combination See *letter combination*.

word A unit of meaning in language.

word analysis To break apart words into parts or individual sounds in order to parse them.

word boundaries The white space that appears before the first letter and after the last letter of a word and that defines the letter or letters as a word. It is important for young readers to learn to recognize word boundaries.

word-by-word matching Usually applied to a beginning reader's ability to match one spoken word with one printed word while reading and pointing. In older readers, the eyes take over the process.

word family A term often used to designate words that are connected by phonograms or rimes (e.g., *hot, not, pot, shot*). A word family can also be a series of words connected by meaning (e.g., *baseless, baseline, baseboard*).

word meaning / vocabulary *Word meaning* refers to the commonly accepted meaning of a word in oral or written language. *Vocabulary* often refers to the words one knows in oral language. *Reading vocabulary*

refers to the words a person can read with understanding.

word origins The ancestry of a word in English and other languages.

word root A word part, usually from another language, that carries the essential meaning of and is the basis for an English word: e.g., *flect, reflect*. Most word roots cannot stand on their own as English words. Some word roots can be combined with affixes to create English words. Compare to *base word*. See also *Greek root, Latin root*.

word structure The parts that make up a word.

words (as a text characteristic) Decodability of words in a text; phonetic and structural features of words.

word-solving actions The strategies a reader uses to recognize words and understand their meaning(s).